Rick Steves

SNAPSHOT

Berlin

CONTENTS

INTRODUCTION

This Snapshot guide, excerpted from my guidebook *Rick Steves'* *Germany,* introduces you to the resurgent German capital. Once divided, now reunited, vibrant Berlin is racing into the future and re-emerging as one of Europe's leading cities. Walk under the Brandenburg Gate and stroll up the boulevard called Unter den Linden, pondering the layers of history beneath your feet. Relive the Cold War as you follow the course of the long-gone Berlin Wall, while towering cranes above you erect glittering new sky-scrapers. Dip into art museums for a look at classical antiquities and the famous bust of Queen Nefertiti. Then take a day-trip to Frederick the Great's palaces and gardens in Potsdam or the sober-ing concentration camp memorial at Sachsenhausen.

To help you have the best trip possible, I've included the fol-lowing topics in this book:

• **Planning Your Time,** with advice on how to make the most of your limited time

• **Orientation,** including tourist information (abbreviated as TI), tips on public transportation, local tour options, and helpful hints

• **Sights** with ratings:

▲▲▲—Don't miss

▲▲—Try hard to see

▲—Worthwhile if you can make it

No rating—Worth knowing about

• **Sleeping** and **Eating,** with good-value recommendations in every price range

• **Connections,** with tips on trains, buses, and driving

Practicalities, near the end of this book, has information on money, phoning, hotel reservations, transportation, and more, plus German survival phrases.

To travel smartly, read this little book in its entirety before you go. It's my hope that this guide will make your trip more meaningful and rewarding. Traveling like a temporary local, you'll get the absolute most out of every mile, minute, and dollar.

Gute Reise!

Rick Steves

BERLIN

No tour of Germany is complete without a look at its historic and reunited capital. Over the last two decades, Berlin has been a construction zone. Standing on ripped-up tracks and under a canopy of cranes, visitors witnessed the rebirth of a great European capital. Although construction continues, today the once-divided city is thoroughly woven back together. Berlin has emerged as one of Europe's top destinations: captivating, lively, fun loving, all-around enjoyable—and easy on the budget.

As you enjoy the thrill of walking over what was the Wall and through the well-patched Brandenburg Gate, it's clear that history is not contained in some book; it's an exciting story of which we are a part. In Berlin, the fine line between history and current events is excitingly blurry.

But even for non-historians, Berlin is a city of fine experiences. Explore the fun and funky neighborhoods emerging in the former East, packed with creative hipster eateries and boutiques trying to one-up each other. Go for a pedal or a cruise along the delightful Spree riverfront. In the city's world-class museums, stroll up the steps of a classical Greek temple amid rough-and-tumble ancient statuary, and peruse canvases by Dürer, Rembrandt, and Vermeer. Nurse a stein of brew in a rollicking beer hall, or dive into a cheap *Currywurst*. On the outskirts of town, at Potsdam, glide like a swan through the opulent halls of an imperial palace, and ponder the darkest chapter of this nation's history at the Sachsenhausen Concentration Camp Memorial (both covered in the next chapter).

Of course, Berlin is still largely defined by its tumultuous 20th century. The city was Hitler's capital during World War II, and in the postwar years, Berlin became the front line of a new

Berlin Sightseeing Modules

Spree River

To Sachsenhausen

EASTERN BERLIN

German Hist. Museum
Museum Island
TV Tower
New Synagogue
Prenzlauer Berg
Berlin Wall Memorial

Reichstag
Brandenburg Gate
Memorial to
  Murdered Jews
Hauptbahnhof

UNTER DEN LINDEN

Checkpoint Charlie
Gendarmenmarkt
Jewish Museum
Topography of Terror

To Potsdam

Bus #100

KU'DAMM

WESTERN BERLIN

Zoo Station
Savignyplatz
  Hotel Area
KaDeWe Dep't Store

CENTRAL BERLIN

Tiergarten Park
Potsdamer Platz
Kulturforum
Gemäldegalerie

global war—one between Soviet-style communism and American-style capitalism. The East-West division was set in stone in 1961, when the East German government boxed in West Berlin with the Berlin Wall. The Wall stood for 28 years. In 1990, less than a year after the Wall fell, the two Germanys—and the two Berlins—officially became one. When the dust settled, Berliners from both sides of the once-divided city faced the monumental challenge of reunification.

Berliners joke that they don't need to travel anywhere because their city's always changing. Spin a postcard rack to see what's new. A 10-year-old guidebook on Berlin covers a different city. City planners have seized on the city's reunification and the return of the national government to make Berlin a great capital once again. When the Wall fell, the East was a decrepit wasteland and the West was a paragon of commerce and materialism. A quarter-century later, the roles are reversed: It's eastern Berlin where you feel the vibrant pulse of the city, while western Berlin seems like yesterday's news.

Berlin today is like the nuclear fuel rod of a great nation. It's vibrant with youth, energy, and an anything-goes-and-anything's-possible buzz (Munich feels spent in comparison). Berlin is both extremely popular and surprisingly affordable. As a booming tourist draw, Berlin claims to be Europe's number-three attraction—now welcoming more visitors annually than Rome.

The History of Berlin

Berlin was a humble, marshy burg—its name perhaps derived from an old Slavic word for "swamp"—until prince electors from the Hohenzollern dynasty made it their capital in the mid-15th century. Gradually their territory spread and strengthened, becoming the powerful Kingdom of Prussia in 1701. As the leading city of Prussia, Berlin dominated the northern Germanic world—both militarily and culturally—long before there was a united "Germany."

The only Hohenzollern ruler worth remembering was Frederick the Great (1712-1786). The ultimate enlightened despot, he was both a ruthless military tactician (he consolidated his kingdom's holdings, successfully invading Silesia and biting off a chunk of Poland) and a cultured lover of the arts (he actively invited artists, architects, and other thinkers to his lands). "Old Fritz," as he was called, played the flute, spoke six languages, and counted Voltaire among his friends. Practical and cosmopolitan, Frederick cleverly invited to Prussia Protestants who were being persecuted elsewhere in Europe—including the French Huguenots and Dutch traders. Prussia became the beneficiary of these groups' substantial wealth and know-how. Frederick the Great left Berlin—and Prussia—a far more modern and enlightened place than he found it. Thanks largely to him, Prussia was well-positioned to become a magnet of sorts for the German unification movement in the 19th century.

When Germany first unified, in 1871, Berlin (as the main city of its most powerful constituent state, Prussia) was its natural capital. Even in the disarray of post-WWI Germany, Berlin thrived as an anything-goes, cabaret-crazy cultural capital of the Roaring '20s. During World War II, the city was Hitler's headquarters—and the place where the Führer drew his final breath. When the Soviet Army reached Berlin in 1945, the protracted fighting left the city in ruins.

Planning Your Time

On all but the shortest trips through Germany, I'd give Berlin three nights and at least two full days, and spend them this way:

Day 1: Begin your day getting oriented to this huge city. For a quick and relaxing once-over-lightly tour, jump on one of the many hop-on, hop-off buses that make two-hour narrated orientation loops through the city. Use the bus to get off and on at places of interest (such as Potsdamer Platz). Then walk from the Reichstag (reservations required), under the Brandenburg Gate, and down Unter den Linden. Tour the German History Museum, and cap your sightseeing day by catching a one-hour boat tour (or pedaling a rented bike) along the park-like banks of the Spree River from Museum Island to the Chancellery.

Day 2: Spend your morning touring the great museums on

After World War II, Berlin was divided by the victorious Allied powers. The American, British, and French sectors became West Berlin, and the Soviet sector, East Berlin. In 1948 and 1949, the Soviets tried to starve the 2.2 million residents of the Western half in an almost medieval-style siege, blockading all roads in and out. But they were foiled by the Berlin Airlift, with the Western Allies flying in supplies from Frankfurt 24 hours a day for 10 months.

Years later, with the overnight construction of the Berlin Wall in 1961, an Iron (or, at least, concrete) Curtain literally cut through the middle of the city, completely encircling West Berlin. For details, see "The Berlin Wall (and Its Fall)" on page 68.

While the wild night when the Wall came down (November 9, 1989) was inspiring, Berlin still faced a fitful transition to reunification. Two cities—and countries—became one at a staggering pace. Reunification had its downside, and the Wall survives in the minds of some people. Some "Ossies" (impolite slang for Easterners) miss their security. Some "Wessies" miss their easy ride (military deferrals, subsidized rent, and tax breaks for living in an isolated city surrounded by the communist world). For free spirits, walled-in West Berlin was a citadel of freedom within the East.

But in recent years, the old East-West division has faded more and more into the background. Ossi-Wessi conflicts no longer dominate the city's political discourse. The city government has been eager to charge forward, with little nostalgia for anything that was associated with the East. Big corporations and the national government have moved in, and the dreary swath of land that was the Wall and its notorious "death strip" has been transformed (as the cash-starved city has been selling off lots of land to anyone determined to develop it). Berlin is a whole new city—ready to welcome visitors.

Museum Island (note that the island's biggest draw, the Pergamon Museum, will be partly closed for the next few years). Dedicate your afternoon to sights of the Third Reich and Holocaust: After lunch, hike via Potsdamer Platz to the Topography of Terror exhibit and along the surviving Niederkirchnerstrasse stretch of the Wall to Checkpoint Charlie. You could also head up to the Berlin Wall Memorial for a more in-depth survey of that infamous barrier, or swing by the Jewish Museum. Finish your day in the lively East—ideally in the once glum, then edgy, now fun-loving and trendy Prenzlauer Berg district.

Berlin merits additional time if you have it. There's much more in the city (such as the wonderful Gemäldegalerie art museum). And nearby are some very worthwhile side-trips: the concentration camp memorial at Sachsenhausen, the palaces at Potsdam (both covered in the next chapter), and the historic town of Wittenberg (which is gearing up for the 500th birthday of the Reformation in 2017).

Orientation to Berlin

Berlin is huge, with 3.4 million people. The city is spread out and its sights numerous, so you'll need to be well-organized to experience the city smartly. The tourist's Berlin can be broken into three main digestible chunks:

1. Eastern Berlin has the highest concentration of notable sights and colorful neighborhoods. Near the landmark Brandenburg Gate, you'll find the Reichstag building, Pariser Platz, and poignant memorials to the victims of Hitler (Jews, Roma and Sinti, and homosexuals). From the Brandenburg Gate, the famous Unter den Linden boulevard runs eastward through former East Berlin, passing the German History Museum (a history lover's favorite) and Museum Island (Pergamon Museum, Neues Museum, and Berlin Cathedral) on the way to Alexanderplatz (TV Tower). The intersection of Unter den Linden and Friedrichstrasse has reclaimed its place as the center of the city. South of Unter den Linden are the delightful Gendarmenmarkt square, most Nazi sites (including the Topography of Terror), some good Wall-related sights (Museum of the Wall at Checkpoint Charlie and East Side Gallery), the Jewish Museum, and the colorful Turkish neighborhood of Kreuzberg. North of Unter den Linden are these worth-a-wander neighborhoods: Oranienburger Strasse (Jewish Quarter and New Synagogue), Hackescher Markt, and Prenzlauer Berg (several recommended hotels and a very lively restaurant/nightlife zone). Just west of Prenzlauer Berg is the Berlin Wall Memorial (with an intact surviving section of the Wall). Eastern Berlin's pedestrian-friendly Spree riverbank is also worth a stroll (or a river cruise).

2. Central Berlin is dominated by the giant Tiergarten park. South of the park are Potsdamer Platz and the Kulturforum museum cluster (including the Gemäldegalerie, New National Gallery, Musical Instruments Museum, and Philharmonic Concert Hall). To the north, the huge Hauptbahnhof (main train station) straddles the former Wall in what was central Berlin's no-man's-land.

3. Western Berlin centers on the Bahnhof Zoo (Zoo train station, often marked "Zoologischer Garten" on transit maps) and the grand Kurfürstendamm boulevard, nicknamed "Ku'damm" (transportation hub, tours, information, shopping, and recommended hotels). The East is all the rage. But the West, while staid in comparison, is bouncing back—with big-name stores and destination restaurants that keep the area buzzing. During the Cold War, this

"Western Sector" was the hub for Western visitors. Capitalists visited the West, with a nervous side-trip beyond the Wall into the grim and foreboding East. (Cubans, Russians, Poles, and Angolans stayed behind the Wall and did their sightseeing in the East.)

Tourist Information

With any luck, you won't have to use Berlin's TIs—they're for-profit agencies working for the city's big hotels, which colors the information they provide. TI branches, appropriately called "info-stores," are unlikely to have the information you need (tel. 030/250-025, www.visitberlin.de). You'll find them at the **Hauptbahnhof** train station (daily 8:00-22:00, by main entrance on Europaplatz), **Ku'damm** (Kurfürstendamm 22, in the glass-and-steel Neues Kranzler Eck building, Mon-Sat 9:30-20:00, Sun 10:00-18:00), and at the **Brandenburg Gate** (daily 9:30-19:00).

Skip the TI's €1 map, and instead pick up any of the walking tour companies' brochures—they include nearly-as-good maps for free. Most hotels also provide free city maps. While the TI does sell the three-day Museumspass (described next), it's also available at major museums. If you take a walking tour, your guide is likely a better source of nightlife or shopping tips than the TI.

Museum Passes: The three-day, €24 **Museumspass** is a great value. It gets you into more than 50 museums, including the national museums and most of the recommended biggies, on three consecutive days. As you'll routinely spend €10-14 per admission, this pays for itself in a hurry. And you'll enjoy the ease of popping in and out of museums that you might not otherwise want to pay for. Buy it at the TI or any participating museum. The pass generally lets you skip the line and go directly into the museum. The €18 **Museum Island Pass** (Bereichskarte Museumsinsel; does not include special exhibits) covers all the venues on Museum Island (otherwise €10-14 each) and is a fine value—but for just €6 more, the three-day Museumspass gives you triple the days and many more entries. TIs also sell the **WelcomeCard,** a transportation pass that also includes some museum discounts (described later, under "Getting Around Berlin").

Local Publications: Various magazines can help make your time in Berlin more productive (available at the TI and/or many newsstands). *Berlin Programm* is a comprehensive German-language monthly, especially strong in high culture, that lists upcoming events and museum hours (€2, www.berlin-programm.de). *Exberliner Magazine,* an English monthly (published mostly by expat Brits who love to poke fun at expat Americans), is very helpful for curious travelers. With a youthful focus, it gives a fascinating insider's look at this fast-changing city (€3 but often given away at theaters or on the street, www.exberliner.com).

Arrival in Berlin
By Train at Berlin Hauptbahnhof

Berlin's newest and grandest train station is Berlin Hauptbahnhof (main train station, a.k.a. "der Bahnhof", abbreviated Hbf). All long-distance trains arrive here, at Europe's biggest, mostly underground train station. This is a "transfer station"—unique for its major lines coming in at right angles—where the national train system meets the city's S-Bahn train system.

The gigantic station can be intimidating, but it's laid out logically on five floors (which, confusingly, can be marked in different ways). Escalators and elevators connect the **main floor** (*Erdgeschoss*, EG, a.k.a. level 0); the two **lower levels** (*Untergeschoss*, UG1 and UG2, a.k.a. levels -1 and -2); and the two **upper levels** (*Obersgeschoss*, OG1 and OG2, a.k.a. levels +1 and +2). Tracks 1-8 are in the lowest underground level (UG2), while tracks 11-16 (along with the S-Bahn) are on the top floor (OG2). Shops and services are concentrated on the three middle levels (EG, OG1, and UG1). The south entrance (toward the Reichstag and downtown, with a taxi stand) is marked *Washingtonplatz*, while the north entrance is marked *Europaplatz*.

Services: On the main floor (EG), you'll find the **TI** (facing the north/*Europaplatz* entrance, look left) and the **"Rail & Fresh WC"** facility (public pay toilets, near the Burger King and food court). Up one level (OG1) is a 24-hour **pharmacy** and the Gepäck Center, where you can securely store your **luggage** (€5/day per bag, daily 6:00-22:00, directly under track 14). Luggage lockers (€4) are difficult to find since they're in the parking garage (levels P-1, P-2, and P-3; look for the garage entrance near Kaisers supermarket on the underground shopping level UG1).

Train Information and Tickets: The station has a Deutsche Bahn *Reisezentrum* information center on the lower level (UG1/-1, daily 6:00-22:00. If you're staying in western Berlin, keep in mind that the info center at the Bahnhof Zoo station is just as good and much less crowded.

EurAide is an English-speaking information desk with answers to your questions about train travel around Europe. It's located right next to the Deutsche Bahn *Reisezentrum* in the underground shopping level (follow signs to tracks 5-6 and *Reisezentrum -1*). It's American-run, so communication is simple. This is an especially good place to make fast-train and *couchette* reservations for later in your trip (April-Sept Mon-Fri 11:00-20:00—though May-July opens at 10:00, closed Sat-Sun; off-season Mon-Fri 11:00-18:30 only and closed Jan-Feb; www.euraide.com).

Shopping: In addition to all those trains, the Hauptbahnhof is home to 80 shops with long hours—some locals call the station a "shopping mall with trains" (daily 8:00-22:00, only stores selling travel provisions are open Sun). The Kaisers supermarket (UG1, follow signs for tracks 1-2) is handy for assembling a picnic for your train ride.

Getting into Town: Taxis and buses wait outside the station, but the S-Bahn is probably the best means of connecting to your destination within Berlin. The crosstown express S-Bahn line connects the station with my recommended hotels in a few minutes. It's simple: All S-Bahn trains are on tracks 15 and 16 at the top of the station (level OG2/+2). All trains on track 15 go east, stopping at Friedrichstrasse, Hackescher Markt (with connections to Prenzlauer Berg), Alexanderplatz, and Ostbahnhof; trains on track 16 go west, toward Bahnhof Zoo and Savignyplatz. (Your train ticket or railpass into the station covers your connecting S-Bahn ride into town; your outbound ticket includes the transfer via S-Bahn to the Hauptbahnhof.)

If you're sleeping at one of my recommended hotels in eastern Berlin's Prenzlauer Berg neighborhood, take any train on track 15 two stops to Hackescher Markt, exit to Spandauer Strasse, go left, and cross the tracks to the tram stop. Here you'll catch tram #M1 north (direction Schillerstrasse).

To reach my recommended hotels in western Berlin, catch any train on track 16 to Savignyplatz, and you're a five-minute walk from your hotel. Savignyplatz is one stop after **Bahnhof Zoo** (rhymes with "toe"; a.k.a. Bahnhof Zoologischer Garten), the once-grand train hub now eclipsed by the Hauptbahnhof. Nowadays Bahnhof Zoo is useful mainly for its shops, uncrowded train-information desk, and BVG public-transit office (outside the entrance, amid the traffic).

The Berlin Hauptbahnhof is not well-connected to the city's U-Bahn (subway) system—yet. The station's sole U-Bahn line—U55—goes only two stops, to the Brandenburger Tor station, and doesn't really connect to the rest of the system. It's part of a planned extension of the U5 line to Alexanderplatz that's far from completion. But for transit junkies, it is an interesting ride on Europe's shortest subway line.

Hauptbahnhof Chaos in 2014: Because Berlin's grand central station was rushed to completion for the 2006 World Cup, its roofline was not finished according to the architect's vision. He sued the owner, Deutsche Bahn, and won. Now the railway is legally obligated to extend the roof. Because of that, the station is suddenly unfinished again. Be warned that, for the near future, it will be under further construction, and many rail travelers will likely be using Bahnhof Zoo and the Ostbahnhof (like in the old days). As both of these are on the S-Bahn line described above, connecting to your hotel should be easy (see "Getting into Town," earlier).

By Plane

For information on reaching the city center from Berlin's airports, see "Berlin Connections" at the end of this chapter.

Helpful Hints

Medical Help: "Call a doc" is a nonprofit referral service designed for tourists (tel. 01805-321-303, phone answered 24 hours a day, www.calladoc.com). Payment is arranged between you and the doctor, and is likely more affordable than similar care in the US. The US Embassy also has a list of local English-speaking doctors (tel. 030/83050, www.usembassy.de).

Museum Tips: Some major Berlin museums are closed on Monday—if you're in town on that day, review hours carefully before making plans. If you plan to see several museums, you'll save money with the Museumspass, which covers nearly all the city sights for three days—including everything covered by the one-day Museum Island Pass (see "Tourist Information—Museum Passes," earlier).

Addresses: Many Berlin streets are numbered with odd and even numbers on the same side of the street, often with no connection to the other side (for example, Ku'damm #212 can be across the street from #14). To save steps, check the white street signs on curb corners; many list the street numbers covered on that side of the block.

Cold War Terminology: Cold War history is important here, so it's helpful to learn a few key terms. What Americans called "East Germany" was technically the German Democratic Republic—the Deutsche Demokratische Republik, or **DDR** (day-day-AIR). You'll still see those initials around what was once East Germany. The formal name for "West Germany" was the Federal Republic of Germany—the

Bundesrepublik Deutschland (BRD)—and is the name now shared by all of reunited Germany.

Internet Access: You'll find Wi-Fi in most hotels and hostels, as well as at small Internet cafés all over the city. In eastern Berlin, try **Hotdog World** in Prenzlauer Berg (Weinbergsweg 4, just a few steps from U8: Rosenthaler Platz toward Kastanienallee), or **Surf Inn** at Alexanderplatz 9. Bahnhof Zoo, Friedrichstrasse, and Hauptbahnhof train stations have coin-operated Internet terminals.

Bookstore: Berlin Story, a big, cluttered, fun bookshop, has a knowledgeable staff and the best selection anywhere in town of English-language books and helpful magazines on Berlin. They also stock an amusing mix of knickknacks and East Berlin nostalgia souvenirs (Mon-Sat 10:00-19:00, Sun 10:00-18:00, Unter den Linden 40, tel. 030/2045-3842, www.berlinstory.de).

Other Berlin Souvenirs: If you're taken with the city's unofficial mascot, the *Ampelmännchen* (traffic-light man), you'll find a world of souvenirs slathered with his iconic red and green image at **Ampelmann Shops** (various locations, including near Gendarmenmarkt at Markgrafenstrasse 37, near Museum Island inside the DomAquarée mall, in the Hackesche Höfe, and at Potsdamer Platz).

Laundry: Berlin has several self-service launderettes with long hours (wash and dry-€4-9/load). Near my recommended hotels in Prenzlauer Berg, try **Waschsalon 115** (daily 6:00-22:00, exact change required, free Wi-Fi, Torstrasse 115, around the corner from the recommended Circus hostel) or **Eco-Express Waschsalon** (daily 6:00-23:00, handy pizzeria next door, Danziger Strasse 7). The **Schnell & Sauber Waschcenter** chain has a location in Prenzlauer Berg (daily 6:00-23:00, exact change required, Oderberger Strasse 1).

Shell Games: Believe it or not, there are still enough idiots on the street to keep the conmen with their shell games in business. Don't be foolish enough to engage with any gambling on the street.

Updates to this Book: For news about changes to this book's coverage since it was published, see www.ricksteves.com/update.

Getting Around Berlin

The city is vast. Berlin's sights spread far and wide. Right from the start, commit yourself to the city's fine public-transit system.

By Public Transit: Subway, Train, Tram, and Bus

Berlin's consolidated transit system uses the same ticket for its many modes of transportation: U-Bahn (*Untergrund-Bahn*, Berlin's subway), S-Bahn (*Stadtschnellbahn*, or "fast urban train," mostly aboveground and with fewer stops), *Strassenbahn* (streetcars, called "trams" by locals), and buses. For all types of transit, there are three lettered zones (A, B, and C). Most of your sightseeing will be in zones A and B (the city proper)—but you'll need to buy a ticket that also covers zone C if you're going to Potsdam, Sachsenhausen, the airport, or other outlying areas.

Ticket Options:

• The €2.40 **basic** ticket *(Einzelfahrschein)* covers two hours of travel in one direction on buses or subways. It's easy to make this ticket stretch to cover several rides...as long as they're in the same direction.

• The €1.40 **short-ride** ticket *(Kurzstrecke)* covers a single ride of six bus stops or three subway stations (one transfer allowed).

• The €8.40 **four-trip** ticket *(4-Fahrten-Karte)* is the same as four basic tickets at a small discount.

• The **day pass** *(Tageskarte)* is good until 3:00 the morning after you buy it (€6.50 for zones AB, €7 for zones ABC). For longer stays, consider a seven-day pass *(Sieben-Tage-Karte;* €28 for zones AB, €34.60 for zones ABC), or the WelcomeCard (described below), which is good for up to five days and also includes sightseeing discounts. The *Kleingruppenkarte* lets groups of up to five travel all day (€15.50 for zones AB, €16 for zones ABC).

• If you've already bought a ticket for zones A and B, and later decide that you also want to go to zone C (such as to Potsdam), you can buy an **"extension ticket"** *(Anschlussfahrschein)* for €1.60 per ride in that zone.

• If you plan to cover a lot of ground using public transportation during a two- or three-day visit, the **WelcomeCard** (available at TIs) is usually the best deal. For longer stays, there's even a five-day option. It covers all public transportation and gives you up to 50 percent discounts on lots of minor and a few major museums (including Checkpoint Charlie), sightseeing tours (including 25 percent off the recommended Original Berlin Walks), and music and theater events (www.visitberlin.de/welcomecard). If you plan to stay inside the city, the Berlin-only option works best (covers transit zones AB, €18.50/48 hours, €24.50/72 hours). For trips beyond the city center, you might want to get the Berlin-with-Potsdam option (zones ABC, €20.50/48 hours, €26.50/72 hours). If you're a museum junkie, consider the **WelcomeCard+Museumsinsel** (€34/72 hours), which combines travel in zones A and B with unlimited access to the five museums on Museum Island. Families get an extra price break: The ABC version (€36/72 hours) is valid for one adult and up to three kids younger than 15.

Buying Tickets: You can buy U-Bahn/S-Bahn tickets from machines at stations. (They are also sold at BVG pavilions at train stations and the TI, from machines on board trams, and on buses from drivers, who'll give change.) *Erwachsener* means "adult"—anyone 14 or older. Don't be afraid of the automated machines: First select the type of ticket you want, then load the coins or paper bills. (Coins work better, so keep some handy.) As you board the bus or tram, or enter the subway system, punch your ticket in a clock machine to validate it (or risk a €50 fine; for an all-day or multiday pass, stamp it only the first time you ride). Be sure to travel with a valid ticket. Tickets are checked frequently, often by plainclothes inspectors. Within Berlin, Eurail passes are good only on S-Bahn connections from the train station when you arrive and to the station when you depart.

Transit Tips: The S-Bahn crosstown express is a river of public transit through the heart of the city, in which many lines converge on one basic highway. Get used to this, and you'll leap within a few minutes between key locations: Savignyplatz (hotels in western Berlin), Bahnhof Zoo (Ku'damm, bus #100), Hauptbahnhof (all major trains in and out of Berlin—unless construction has temporarily re-routed some), Friedrichstrasse (a short walk north of the heart of Unter den Linden; this station has the interesting Palace of Tears exhibit), Hackescher Markt (Museum Island, restaurants, nightlife, connection to Prenzlauer Berg hotels and eateries), and Alexanderplatz (eastern end of Unter den Linden).

Sections of the U-Bahn or S-Bahn sometimes close temporarily for repairs. In this situation, a bus route often replaces the train (*Ersatzverkehr,* or "replacement transportation"; *zwischen* means "between").

Berlin's public transit is operated by BVG (except the S-Bahn, run by Deutsche Bahn). Schedules, including bus timetables, are available on the helpful BVG website (www.bvg.de). Get and use the excellent *Discover Berlin by Train and Bus* map-guide published by BVG (at subway ticket windows).

By Taxi

Cabs are easy to flag down, and taxi stands are common. A typical ride within town costs €8-10, and a crosstown trip (for example, Bahnhof Zoo to Alexanderplatz) will run about €15. Tariff 1 is for a *Kurzstrecke* (see below). All other rides are tariff 2 (€3.20 drop plus €1.65/kilometer for the first 7 kilometers, then €1.28/kilometer after that). If possible, use cash—paying with a credit card comes with a hefty surcharge (about €4, regardless of the fare).

Money-Saving Taxi Tip: For any ride of less than two kilometers (about a mile), you can save several euros if you take advantage of the **Kurzstrecke** (short-stretch) rate. To get this rate, it's important that you flag the cab down on the street—not at or even near a taxi stand. Also, you must ask for the *Kurzstrecke* rate as soon as you hop in: Confidently say *"Kurzstrecke, bitte"* (KOORTS-shtreh-keh, BIT-teh), and your driver will grumble and flip the meter to a fixed €4 rate (for a ride that would otherwise cost €7).

By Bike

Flat Berlin is a very bike-friendly city, but be careful—Berlin's motorists don't brake for bicyclists (and bicyclists don't brake for pedestrians). Fortunately, some roads and sidewalks have special red-painted bike lanes. Don't ride on the regular sidewalk—it's *verboten* (though locals do it all the time). Better yet, to get out of the city on two wheels, rent a bike, take it on the subway (requires extra €1.60 ticket) to the pleasant Potsdam/Wannsee parkland area west of town, then ride through forests and along skinny lakes to the vast Grünewald park, then back into the city. (Back during the Cold War, Grünewald was the Wessies' playground, while Ossies communed with nature at the Müggelsee east of town.) Bike shops can suggest a specific route.

Fat Tire Bikes rents good bikes at two handy locations—East (at the base of the TV Tower near Alexanderplatz—facing the entrance to the tower, go around to the right) and West (at Bahnhof Zoo—leaving the station onto Hardenbergplatz, turn left and walk 100 yards to the big bike sign). Both locations have the same hours and rates (€7/4 hours, €12/day, cheaper rate for two or more days, free luggage storage and Internet access, daily May-Sept 9:30-20:00, March-April and Oct-Nov 9:30-18:00, shorter hours or by appointment only Dec-Feb, leave ID, tel. 030/2404-7991, www.berlinbikerental.com).

In eastern Berlin, **Take a Bike**—near the Friedrichstrasse S-Bahn station—is owned by a lovely Dutch-German couple who know a lot about bikes and have a huge inventory. They can help you find the perfect fit (3-gear bikes: €8/4 hours, €12.50/day, €19/2 days, slightly cheaper for longer rentals, more for better bikes, electric bikes-€29/day, helmets, daily 9:30-19:00, Neustädtische Kirchstrasse 8, tel. 030/2065-4730, www.takeabike.de). To find it, leave the S-Bahn station via the Friedrichstrasse exit, turn right, go through a triangle-shaped square, and hang a left on Neustädtische Kirchstrasse.

Tours in Berlin

▲▲▲Hop-on, Hop-off Bus Tours

Several companies offer the same routine: a €12-15 circuit of the city with unlimited hop-on, hop-off privileges all day (about 15 stops at the city's major sights) on buses with cursory narration in English and German by a live, sometimes tired guide or a boring

Berlin at a Glance

▲▲▲**German History Museum** The ultimate swing through Germany's tumultuous story. **Hours:** Daily 10:00-18:00. See page 50.

▲▲▲**Pergamon Museum** World-class museum of classical antiquities on Museum Island, featuring the fantastic second-century B.C. Greek Pergamon Altar and frieze—which will close for a multi-year restoration in the fall of 2014. **Hours:** Daily 10:00-18:00, Thu until 20:00. See page 53.

▲▲**Reichstag** Germany's historic parliament building, topped with a striking modern dome you can climb (reservations required). **Hours:** Daily 8:00-24:00, last entry at 22:00. See page 25.

▲▲**Brandenburg Gate** One of Berlin's most famous landmarks, a massive columned gateway, at the former border of East and West. **Hours:** Always open. See page 29.

▲▲**Memorial to the Murdered Jews of Europe** Holocaust memorial with almost 3,000 symbolic pillars, plus an exhibition about Hitler's Jewish victims. **Hours:** Memorial always open; information center open Tue-Sun 10:00-20:00, Oct-March until 19:00, closed Mon. See page 32.

▲▲**Unter den Linden** Leafy boulevard through the heart of former East Berlin, lined with some of the city's top sights. **Hours:** Always open. See page 35.

▲▲**Neues Museum** Egyptian antiquities collection (on Museum Island) and proud home of the exquisite 3,000-year-old bust of Queen Nefertiti. **Hours:** Daily 10:00-18:00, Thu until 20:00. See page 56.

▲▲**Gendarmenmarkt** Inviting square bounded by twin churches (one with a fine German history exhibit), a chocolate shop, and a concert hall. **Hours:** Always open. See page 61.

▲▲**Topography of Terror** Chilling exhibit documenting the Nazi perpetrators, built on the site of the former Gestapo/SS headquarters. **Hours:** Daily 10:00-20:00. See page 63.

▲▲**Museum of the Wall at Checkpoint Charlie** Kitschy but moving museum with stories of brave Cold War escapes, near the former site of the famous East-West border checkpoint; the surrounding street scene is almost as interesting. **Hours:** Daily 9:30-22:00. See page 70.

▲▲**Jewish Museum Berlin** Engaging, accessible museum celebrating Jewish culture, in a highly conceptual building. **Hours:** Daily 10:00-20:00, Mon until 22:00. See page 71.

▲▲**Gemäldegalerie** Germany's top collection of 13th- through 18th-century European paintings, featuring Holbein, Dürer, Cranach, Van der Weyden, Rubens, Hals, Rembrandt, Vermeer, Velázquez, Raphael, and more. **Hours:** Tue-Sun 10:00-18:00, Thu until 20:00, closed Mon. See page 89.

▲▲**Berlin Wall Memorial** A "docu-center" with videos and displays, several outdoor exhibits, and lone surviving stretch of an intact Wall section. **Hours:** Visitor Center April-Oct Tue-Sun 9:30-19:00, Nov-March until 18:00, closed Mon; outdoor areas accessible 24 hours daily. See page 78.

▲**Old National Gallery** German paintings, mostly from the Romantic Age. **Hours:** Tue-Sun 10:00-18:00, Thu until 20:00, closed Mon. See page 59.

▲**DDR Museum** Quirky collection of communist-era artifacts. **Hours:** Daily 10:00-20:00, Sat until 22:00. See page 43.

▲**New Synagogue** Largest prewar synagogue in Berlin, damaged in World War II, with a rebuilt facade and modest museum. **Hours:** March-Oct Sun-Mon 10:00-20:00, Tue-Thu 10:00-18:00, Fri 10:00-17:00—until 14:00 in March and Oct; Nov-Feb Sun-Thu 10:00-18:00, Fri 10:00-14:00; closed Sat year-round. See page 76.

▲**Potsdamer Platz** The "Times Square" of old Berlin, long a postwar wasteland, now rebuilt with huge glass skyscrapers, an underground train station, and—covered with a huge canopy—the Sony Center mall. **Hours:** Always open. See page 85.

▲**Deutsche Kinemathek Film and TV Museum** An entertaining look at German film and TV, from *Metropolis* to Dietrich to Nazi propaganda to the present day. **Hours:** Tue-Sun 10:00-18:00, Thu until 20:00, closed Mon. See page 87.

▲**Kaiser Wilhelm Memorial Church** Evocative destroyed church in heart of the former West Berlin, with modern annex. **Hours:** Church—daily 9:00-19:00; Memorial Hall in bombed tower—Mon-Sat 10:00-18:00, shorter hours Sun. See page 95.

▲**Käthe Kollwitz Museum** The black-and-white art of the Berlin artist who conveyed the suffering of her city's stormiest century. **Hours:** Daily 11:00-18:00. See page 96.

recorded commentary in whatever language you want to dial up. In season, each company has buses running four times per hour. They are cheap and great for photography—and Berlin really lends itself to this kind of bus-tour orientation. You can hop off at any major tourist spot (Potsdamer Platz, Museum Island, Brandenburg Gate, the Kaiser Wilhelm Memorial Church, and so on). Go with a live guide rather than the recorded spiel (so you get a few current asides). When choosing seats, check the sun/shade situation—some buses are entirely topless, and others are entirely covered. My favorites are topless with a shaded covered section in the back (April-Oct daily 10:00-18:00, last bus leaves all stops at 16:00, 2-hour loop; for specifics, look for brochures in your hotel lobby or at the TI). Keep your ticket so you can hop off and on (with the same company) all day. In winter (Nov-March), buses come only twice an hour, and the last departure is at 15:00. Brochures explain extras offered by each company.

Other Bus Tours

City Bus #100

For do-it-yourselfers, Berlin's city bus #100 is a cheap, quick, workable alternative to the commercial hop-on, hop-off bus tours.

Bus Tours

BEX Sightseeing Berlin offers a long list of bus tours (including hop-on, hop-off) in and around Berlin; their 2.5-hour "City Circle" tour is a good introduction. You can hop on and off at any of 20 stops, or simply stay on for the full tour (€22, ticket good 2 days; April-Oct daily at 10:00, Fri-Sun also at 14:00; Nov-March Wed-Sat at 10:00, no tours Sun-Tue; recorded English commentary provided over earphones, departs from Ku'damm 216, buy ticket at bus, tel. 030/880-4190, www.berlinerstadtrundfahrten.de).

▲▲▲Walking Tours

Berlin's fascinating and complex recent history can be challenging to appreciate on your own, making the city an ideal place to explore with a walking tour. Equal parts historian and entertainer, a good Berlin tour guide makes the city's dynamic story come to life.

But unlike many other European countries, Germany has no regulations controlling who can give city tours. This can make guide quality hit-or-miss, ranging from brilliant history buffs who've lived in Berlin for years while pursuing their PhDs, to new arrivals who memorize a script and start leading tours after being in town for just a couple of weeks. In general you have the best odds of landing a great guide by using one of the more established companies I recommend in this section.

Most outfits offer walks that are variations on the same themes: general **introductory** walk, **Third Reich** walk (Hitler and Nazi sites), and day trips to **Potsdam** and the **Sachsenhausen Concentration Camp Memorial**. Most tours cost about €12-15 and last about three to four hours (longer for the side-trips to Potsdam and Sachsenhausen—for details, see the next chapter); public-transit tickets and entrances to sights are extra. I've included some basic descriptions for each company, but for details—including prices and specific schedules—see the various websites or look for brochures in town (widely available at TIs, hotel reception desks, and many cafés and shops).

Brewer's Berlin Tours

Specializing in longer, more in-depth walks that touch on the entire span of Berlin's past, this company was started by the late, great Terry Brewer, who once worked for the British diplomatic service in East Berlin. Terry left the company to his guides, a group of historians who get very excited about Berlin. Their in-depth tours through the city are intimate, relaxed, and can flex with your interests. Their Best of Berlin introductory tour, billed at six hours, can last for eight (daily at 10:30). They also do a shorter three-hour tour (free, tip expected, daily at 13:00) and an all-day Potsdam tour (Wed and Sat, May-Oct). All tours depart from Bandy Brooks ice cream shop at the Friedrichstrasse S-Bahn station (tel. 030/2248-7435, mobile 0177-388-1537, www.brewersberlintours.com).

Insider Tour

This well-regarded company runs the full gamut of itineraries: introductory walk (daily), Third Reich, Cold War, Jewish Berlin, Sachsenhausen, and Potsdam, as well as bike tours, pub crawls, and a day trip to Dresden. Their tours have two meeting points (some tours convene at both, others at just one—check the schedule): in the West at the McDonald's across from Bahnhof Zoo, and in the East at AM to PM Bar at the Hackescher Markt S-Bahn station (tel. 030/692-3149, www.insidertour.com).

Original Berlin Walks

Their flagship introductory walk, Discover Berlin, offers a good overview in four hours (daily year-round, meet at 10:00 at Bahnhof Zoo, April-Oct also daily at 13:30). They offer a Third Reich walking tour (4/week in summer); tours to Potsdam and Sachsenhausen; and themed walks on Jewish Life in Berlin, Cold War Berlin, and Queer Berlin (each 1/week April-Oct only). Readers of this book get a €1 discount per tour in 2014. All tours meet at the taxi stand in front of the Bahnhof Zoo train station; the Discover Berlin, Jewish Life, and Sachsenhausen tours also have a second departure point opposite the Hackescher Markt S-Bahn station, outside the Weihenstephaner restaurant (tour info: tel. 030/301-9194, www.berlinwalks.de).

Berlin Underground Association (Berliner Unterwelten Verein)

Much of Berlin's history lies beneath the surface, and this group has an exclusive agreement with the city to explore and research what is hidden underground. Their one-of-a-kind Dark Worlds tour of a WWII air-raid bunker features a chilling explanation of the air war over Berlin (Thu-Mon at 11:00). The From Flak Towers to Mountains of Debris tour enters the Humboldthain air defense tower (Thu-Sun at 15:00). The Subways and Bunkers in the Cold War tour visits a completely stocked and fully functional nuclear emergency bunker in former West Berlin (Tue-Sun at 13:00). Additional tour times and days are added in summer; check the schedule online. Each tour costs €10. Meet in the hall of the Gesundbrunnen U-Bahn/S-Bahn station—follow signs to the *Humboldthain/Brunnenstrasse* exit, and walk up the stairs to their office (tel. 030/4991-0517, www.berliner-unterwelten.de).

Alternative Berlin Tours

Specializing in cutting-edge street culture and art, this company emphasizes the bohemian chic that flavors the city's ever-changing urban scene. Their basic three-hour tour (daily at 11:00, 13:00, and 15:00) is tip-based; other tours cost €12 (all tours meet at Starbucks on Alexanderplatz under the TV Tower, mobile 0162-819-8264, www.alternativeberlin.com).

"Free" Tours

You'll see companies advertising supposedly "free" introductory tours all over town. Designed for and popular with students (free is good), it's a business model that has spread across Europe: English-speaking students (often Aussies and Americans) deliver a memorized script before a huge crowd lured in by the promise of a free tour. What the customers don't know is that the guide must turn over about €3 per person to the company, so tour leaders expect to be "tipped in paper" (€5 minimum per person is encouraged). The "free" intro tour is then used to push other tours that do charge a fee. While the guides can be highly entertaining, the better ones typically move on to more serious tour companies before long. These tours are fine for poor students with little interest in real history. But as in many things, when it comes to walking tours, you get what you pay for.

The "free" tour companies also offer **pub crawls** that are wildly popular with visiting college students.

Local Guides

Berlin guides are generally independent contractors who work with the various tour companies (like those listed here). Many of them are Americans who came to town as students and history buffs, fell in love with the city, and now earn their living as guides. Some lead private tours on their own (generally charging around €50/hour or

€200/day, confirm by email when booking). The following guides are all good: **Nick Jackson** (an archaeologist and historian who makes museums come to life, mobile 0171-537-8768, www.jacksonsberlintours.com, info@jacksonsberlintours.com); **Lee Evans** (makes 20th-century Germany a thriller, mobile 0177-423-5307, lee.evans@berlin.de); and **Bernhard Wagner** (mobile 0176-6422-9119, www.steubentoursberlin.com, schlegelmilch@gmx.net).

Bike Tours

Fat Tire Bike Tours

Choose among five different tours, which run (except where noted) from mid-March through October (most €24, 4-6 hours, 6-10 miles): **City Tour** (March-Nov daily at 11:00, May-Sept also daily at 16:00, Dec-Feb Wed and Sat at 11:00), **Berlin Wall Tour** (Mon, Thu, and Sat at 10:30), **Third Reich Tour** (Wed, Fri, and Sun at 10:30), "**Raw**" **Tour** (countercultural, creative aspects of contemporary Berlin, Tue, Fri, and Sun at 10:30), and **Gardens and Palaces of Potsdam Tour** (€42, Wed, Sat, and Sun at 10:00). For any tour, meet at the TV Tower at Alexanderplatz (reserve ahead except for City Tour, tel. 030/2404-7991, www.fattirebiketours.com).

Finding Berlin Tours

This small, easygoing company offers tours that take you away from the mainstream sights and focus on Berlin's neighborhoods, people, and street art (€22-25/person, max 8 people, 3-5 hours, in the Velosaloon bike shop at Schlesische Strasse 29, U-Bahn: Schlesisches Tor, mobile 0176-9933-3913, see schedule at www.findingberlin-tours.com).

Boat Tours

Spree River Cruises

Several boat companies offer one-hour, €11 trips up and down the river. A relaxing hour on one of these boats can be time and money well spent. You'll listen to excellent English audioguides, see lots of wonderful new government-commissioned architecture, and enjoy the lively park action fronting the river. Boats leave from various docks that cluster near the bridge at the Berlin Ca-thedral (just off Unter den Linden). I enjoyed the Historical Sightseeing Cruise from **Stern und Kreisschiffahrt** (mid-March-Nov daily 10:45-19:15, leaves from Nikolaiviertel Dock—cross bridge from Berlin Cathedral toward Alexanderplatz and look right, tel.

030/536-3600, www.sternundkreis.de). Confirm that the boat you choose comes with English commentary.

Self-Guided Bus Tour

Bus #100 from Bahnhof Zoo to Alexanderplatz

While hop-on, hop-off bus tours are a great value, Berlin's city bus #100 laces together the major sights in a kind of poor man's bus tour. Bus #100 stops at Bahnhof Zoo, the Berlin Zoo, Victory Column, Reichstag, Unter den Linden, Brandenburg Gate, Pergamon Museum, and Alexanderplatz. An electronic board inside the bus displays the upcoming stop. As a basic €2.40 bus ticket is good for up to two hours of travel in one direction and buses leave every few minutes, hopping on and off works great. The #100 route is smooth until the Reichstag, but from there, construction projects can cause random detours, making it frustrating to follow the last part of this route (which is better on foot anyway).

Starting in the West from Bahnhof Zoo, here's a quick review of what you'll see: Leaving the train station, on your left and straight ahead, you'll spot the bombed-out hulk of the **Kaiser Wilhelm Memorial Church,** with its postwar sister church. Then, on the left, the elephant gates mark the entrance to the venerable and much-loved **Berlin Zoo** and its aquarium. After a left turn, you cross the canal and pass Berlin's **embassy row.** The first interesting embassy is Mexico's, with columns that seem to move when you're driving by (how do they do that?). The big turquoise wall marks the communal home of all five Nordic embassies. This building is very "green," run entirely on solar power.

The bus then enters the 400-acre **Tiergarten** park, packed with cycling paths, joggers, and—on hot days—nude sunbathers. Straight ahead, the **Victory Column** (Siegessäule; with the gilded angel) towers above this vast city park that was once a royal hunting ground. A block beyond the Victory Column (on the left) is the 18th-century late-Rococo **Bellevue Palace.** Formerly the official residence of the Prussian (and later German) crown prince, and at one time a Nazi VIP guest house, it's now the residence of the federal president (whose power is mostly ceremonial—the chancellor wields the real clout). If the flag's out, he's in.

Driving along the Spree River (on the left), you'll see buildings of the **national government.** The huge brick "brown snake" complex (across the river) was built to house government workers—but it didn't sell, so now its apartments are available to anyone. A metal Henry Moore sculpture entitled *Butterfly* (a.k.a. "The Drinker's Liver") floats in front of the slope-roofed House of World Cultures (Berliners have nicknamed this building "the pregnant oyster" and

"Jimmy Carter's smile"). The modern tower (next, on the left) is a carillon with 68 bells (from 1987). Through the trees on the left you'll see the **Chancellery**—Germany's "White House." The big open space is the **Platz der Republik,** where the Victory Column (which you passed earlier) stood until Hitler moved it. The Hauptbahnhof (Berlin's vast main train station, marked by its tall tower with the *DB* sign) is across the field between the Chancellery and the **Reichstag** (Germany's parliament—the old building with the new dome).

The next string of attractions are best seen on foot (see the "Self-Guided Walk," next). But if you stay on the bus, you'll zip by them in this order:

Unter den Linden, the main east-west thoroughfare, stretches from the **Brandenburg Gate** (behind you) through Berlin's historic core (ahead) to the TV Tower in the distance (Alexanderplatz, where this bus finishes). You'll pass the **Russian Embassy** and the Aeroflot airline office (right). Crossing **Friedrichstrasse,** look right for a Fifth Avenue-style conga line of big, glitzy department stores. Later, on the left, are the **German History Museum, Museum Island**, and the **Berlin Cathedral;** across from these (on the right) is the construction site of the **Humboldt-Forum** (with the Humboldt-Box visitors center). Then you'll rumble to a final stop at what was the center of East Berlin in communist times: **Alexanderplatz.**

Self-Guided Walk

The Best of Berlin

This walk starts in front of the Reichstag, takes you under the Brandenburg Gate and down Unter den Linden, and finishes up on Alexanderplatz, near the TV Tower. I describe minor sights along the way, and also point out major ones that you'll want to see later or by taking a break from the walk (find their details later in the chapter, under "Sights in Eastern Berlin"). If you have just one day in Berlin, simply follow this two-mile walk (two hours at a brisk pace, not counting museum visits), and you'll have seen the core of the city and its most important sights. While you can visit the sights covered here in any order you like, it's most efficient to do them in the context of this walk.

• *Start your walk directly in front of the Reichstag building, at the big park called...*

Platz der Republik

Stand about 100 yards in front of the grand Reichstag building and spin left to survey the surroundings. At the **Reichstag U-Bahn stop** is a big federal building overlooking the Spree River. The huge new

BERLIN

Berlin Self-Guided Walk

500 Kilometers

1/2 Mile

HANNOVERSCHE STR.

ORANIENBURGER

FRIEDRICHSTRASSE

HAUPTBAHNHOF
& EURAIDE

Haupt-bahnhof

Washington Platz

Oranienburger Tor

JOHANNIS-

HUMBOLDTHAFEN

LUISENSTR.

SCHUMANNSTR.

KAPELLE UFER

REINHARD-STR.

ALBRECHTSTR.

ZIEGEL-

Spree River

FÜRST-BISMARCK-STR. (TUNNEL)

MARIENSTR.

AM WEIDEN- DAMM

PLANK-

ALT-MOABIT

ELEVATED RAILWAY

PALACE OF TEARS

Friedrich-strasse

OTTO-VON-BISMARCK-ALLEE

SCHIFFBAUERDAMM

GEORGENSTR.

CHANCELLERY

Bundestag

PARLIAMENT

DOROTHEEN-STR.

STRASSE

FRIEDRICH-

HAUS DER KULTUREN DER WELT

Platz der Republik

REICHSTAG

❷

SCHEIDEMANNSTR.

BUS #100

❸

❶

WALK BEGINS

NEUSTÄDTISCHE KIRCHSTR.

SCHADOW

MITTELSTR.

❶❸

← To Bahnhof Zoo via Bus #100

REICHSTAG VISITORS CENTER

BRANDENBURG GATE

❺

❹

Pariser

UNTER   DEN   LINDEN

STRASSE

To Victory Column

STRASSE DES 17 JUNI

❻

Platz

❼

Branden-burger Tor

KOMISCHE OPER

❶❷

MEMORIAL TO THE MURDERED JEWS OF EUROPE

❽

DZ BANK

ACAD OF ART

HOTEL ADLON

BEHRENSTRASSE

Französische Strasse

····· Former Course of the Wall

❾

HANNAH-ARENDT-STRASSE

GLINKASTR.

MAUERSTR.

JÄGERSTR.

❶❶

Tiergarten

ENTLASTUNGS-

LENNÉSTR.

EBERTSTRASSE

IN DEN MINISTER-GÄRTEN

❶⓪

WILHELMSTR.

TAUBENSTR.

MOHRENSTR.

To Kulturforum

To Potsdamer Platz

VOSSSTR.

U Mohren-strasse

❶ Reichstag
❷ Spree Riverfront
❸ Memorial to Politicians Who Opposed Hitler
❹ Berlin Wall Victims Memorial
❺ Monument to the Murdered Sinti & Roma of Europe
❻ Brandenburg Gate

❼ Pariser Platz
❽ US Embassy
❾ Memorial to the Murdered Jews of Europe
❶⓪ Site of Hitler's Bunker
❶❶ Memorial to the Homosexuals Persecuted Under the National Socialist Regime
❶❷ Russian Embassy

main train station (Hauptbahnhof) is in the distance (see the tower marked *DB*, for Deutsche Bahn—the German rail company). Farther left is the mammoth white concrete-and-glass **Chancellery,** nicknamed the "washing machine" by Berliners for its hygienic, spin-cycle appearance. It's the office of Germany's most powerful person, the chancellor (currently Angela Merkel). To remind the chancellor who he or she works for, Germany's Reichstag (housing the parliament) is about six feet taller than the Chancellery.

• *Dominating the Platz der Republik is a giant domed building, the...*

⑬ Berlin Story Bookstore & Museum
⑭ Bebelplatz
⑮ Humboldt University
⑯ German State Opera
⑰ Neue Wache
⑱ German History Museum
⑲ Museum Island
⑳ Berlin Cathedral
㉑ Humboldt-Box & Forum
㉒ Spree River Cruises
㉓ DDR Museum
㉔ Marien Church
㉕ Women's Protest Memorial
㉖ TV Tower
㉗ Alexanderplatz

▲▲Reichstag

The parliament building—the heart of German democracy—has a short but complicated and emotional history. When it was inaugurated in the 1890s, the last emperor, Kaiser Wilhelm II, disdainfully called it the "chatting home for monkeys" (*Reichsaffenhaus*). It was placed outside the city's old walls—far from the center of real power, the imperial palace. But it was from the Reichstag that the German Republic was proclaimed in 1918. Look above the door, surrounded by stone patches from WWII bomb damage, to see the motto and promise: *Dem Deutschen Volke* ("To the German People").

In 1933, this symbol of democracy nearly burned down. The Nazis—whose influence on the German political scene was on the rise—blamed a communist plot. A Dutch communist, Marinus van der Lubbe, was eventually convicted and guillotined for the crime. Others believed that Hitler himself planned the fire, using it as a handy excuse to frame the communists and grab power. Even though Van der Lubbe was posthumously pardoned by the German government in 2008, most modern historians concede that he most likely was indeed guilty, and had acted alone—the Nazis were just incredibly lucky to have his deed advance their cause.

The Reichstag was hardly used from 1933 to 1999. Despite the fact that the building had lost its symbolic value, Stalin ordered his troops to take the Reichstag from the Nazis no later than May 1, 1945 (the date of the workers' May Day parade in Moscow). More than 1,500 Nazi soldiers made their last stand here—extending World War II by two days. On April 30, after fierce fighting on its rooftop, the Reichstag fell to the Red Army.

For the building's 101st birthday in 1995, the Bulgarian-American artist Christo wrapped it in silvery gold cloth. It was then wrapped again—in scaffolding—and rebuilt by British architect Lord Norman Foster into the new parliamentary home of the Bundestag (Germany's lower house, similar to the US House of Representatives). In 1999, the German parliament convened here for the first time in 66 years. To many Germans, the proud resurrection of the Reichstag symbolizes the end of a terrible chapter in their country's history.

The **glass cupola** rises 155 feet above the ground. Its two sloped ramps spiral 755 feet to the top for a grand view. Inside the dome, a cone of 360 mirrors reflects natural light into the legislative chamber below. Lit from inside after dark, this gives Berlin a memorable nightlight. The environmentally friendly cone—with an opening at the top—also helps with air circulation, expelling stale air from the legislative chamber (no joke) and pulling in fresh, cool air.

Visitors with advance reservations can climb the spiral ramp up into that cupola.

• *Facing the Reichstag, you can take a short side-trip to the river by circling around to the left of the building.*

Spree Riverfront

Admire the wonderful architecture incorporating the Spree River into the people's world. It's a poignant spot because this river was

once a symbol of division—the East German regime put nets underwater to stymie those desperate enough for freedom to swim to the West. When kings ruled Prussia, government buildings went right up to the water. But today, the city is incorporating the river thoughtfully into a people-friendly cityscape. From the Reichstag, a delightful riverside path leads around the curve, past "beach cafés," to the riverbank behind the Chancellery. For a slow, low-impact glide past this zone, consider a river cruise (we'll pass the starting point—on Museum Island—later on this walk). The fine bridges symbolize the connection of East and West.

• *Back in front of the Reichstag, face the building and walk to the right. Near the road in front of the Reichstag, enmeshed in all the security apparatus and crowds, is a memorial of slate stones embedded in the ground.*

Memorial to Politicians Who Opposed Hitler

This row of slabs, which looks like a fancy slate bicycle rack, is a memorial to the 96 members of the Reichstag (the equivalent of our

members of Congress) who were persecuted and murdered because their politics didn't agree with Chancellor Hitler's. They were part of the Weimar Republic, the weak and ill-fated attempt at post-WWI democracy in Germany. These were the people who could have stopped Hitler...so they became his first victims. Each slate slab memorializes one man—his name, party (mostly KPD—Communists, and SPD—Social Democrats), and the date and location of his death—generally in concentration camps. (*KZ* stands for "concentration camp.") They are honored here, in front of the building in which they worked.

• *Walk along the side of the Reichstag, on busy Scheidemannstrasse, toward the rear of the building. At the intersection with Ebertstrasse, cross to the right (toward the park). Along a railing is a small memorial of white crosses. This is the...*

Berlin Wall Victims Memorial

This monument commemorates some of the East Berliners who died trying to cross the Wall. Many of them perished within months of

the Wall's construction on August 13, 1961. Most died trying to swim the river to freedom. The monument used to stand right on the Berlin Wall behind the Reichstag. Notice that the last person killed while trying to escape was 20-year-old Chris Gueffroy, who died nine months before the Wall fell in 1989. (He was shot through the heart in no-man's land.)

• *Continue along Ebertstrasse (away from the Reichstag) for a few more steps and turn into the peaceful lane on the right (into Tiergarten park— more about it in a minute). Within a short distance, on your right, is the...*

Monument to the Murdered Sinti and Roma (Gypsies) of Europe

Unveiled in 2012, this memorial remembers the roughly 500,000 Sinti and Roma victims of the Holocaust. "Sinti" and "Roma" (the main tribes and politically correct terms for the group more commonly called "Gypsies") were as persecuted by the Nazis as were the Jews. And they lost the same percentage of their population to Hitler. The opaque glass wall, with a timeline in English and German, traces the Nazi abuse and atrocities.

Enter through the rusty steel portal. On the other side is a circular reflecting pool surrounded by stone slabs, some containing the names of the death camps where hundreds of thousands of Sinti and Roma perished. In the water along the rim of the pool is the heart-wrenching poem "Auschwitz," by composer and writer Santino Spinelli, an Italian Roma. Dissonant music evoking the tragedy of the Gypsy genocide adds to the atmosphere.

The memorial is relatively humble and unkempt (with algae mucking up the pond). "Do you speak English?" beggar ladies— bussed in by traffickers from Romania—hit up visitors here at their own memorial. It's a chance to appreciate, or at least ponder, the plight and struggles of a fragmented community with a nomadic heritage that refuses to conform to modern norms and has no organizational center or effective leadership.

• *Retrace your steps to Ebertstrasse and turn right, toward the busy intersection dominated by the imposing Brandenburg Gate. You're at one edge of...*

The Brandenburg Gate, Arch of Peace

Two hundred years ago, the Brandenburg Gate was designed as an arch of peace, crowned by the Goddess of Peace and showing Mars sheathing his sword. The Nazis misused it as a gate of triumph and aggression. Today a Room of Silence, built into the gate, is dedicated to the peaceful message of the original Brandenburg Gate (daily 11:00-18:00, shorter hours in winter). As you consider the history of Berlin in this silent and empty room—which is carefully not dedicated to any particular religion—you may be inspired to read the prayer of the United Nations:

"Oh Lord, our planet Earth is only a small star in space. It is our duty to transform it into a planet whose creatures are no longer tormented by war, hunger, and fear, no longer senselessly divided by race, color, and ideology. Give us courage and strength to begin this task today so that our children and our children's children shall one day carry the name of man with pride."

Tiergarten Park

Take this chance to get oriented. Facing the Brandenburg Gate is the park called Tiergarten (considered the "green lungs of Berlin"); its center is marked by the Victory Column (Siegessäule), which originally stood where you started this tour. Hitler had the column moved in the 1930s to its present position in the Tiergarten as the first step in creating the grandiose axis he envisioned for postwar Berlin.

Now face the Brandenburg Gate. It stands at one end of Unter den Linden, the Champs-Elysées of Berlin. In the distance, the red-and-white spire of the TV Tower marks the end of this walk (which, from here, is essentially a straight line with a few little detours).

• *As you cross the street toward the gate, notice the double row of cobblestones beneath your feet—it goes about 25 miles around the city, marking where the Wall used to stand. Then walk under the gate that, for a sad generation, was part of a wall that divided this city.*

▲▲Brandenburg Gate (Brandenburger Tor)

The historic Brandenburg Gate (1791) was the grandest—and is the last survivor—of 14 gates in Berlin's old city wall (this one led to the neighboring city of Brandenburg). The gate was the symbol of Prussian Berlin—and later the symbol of a divided Berlin. It's crowned by a majestic four-horse chariot, with the Goddess of Peace at the reins. Napoleon took this statue to the Louvre in Paris in 1806. After the Prussians defeated Napoleon and got it back

(1813), she was renamed the Goddess of Victory.

The gate sat unused, part of a sad circle dance called the Wall, for more than 25 years. Now postcards all over town show the ecstatic day—November 9, 1989—when the world rejoiced at the sight of happy Berliners jamming the gate like flowers on a parade float. Pause a minute and think about struggles for freedom—past and present. (There's actually a special room built into the gate for this purpose—see the sidebar.) Around the gate, look at the information boards with pictures of how this area changed throughout the 20th century. There's a TI within the gate (S-Bahn: Brandenburger Tor).

The gate sits on a major boulevard running east to west through Berlin. The western segment, called Strasse des 17 Juni (named for a workers' uprising against the DDR government on June 17, 1953), stretches for four miles from the Brandenburg Gate and Victory Column to the Olympic Stadium. But we'll follow this city axis in the opposite direction, east, along Unter den Linden. The walk takes us into the core of old imperial Berlin and past the site where the palace of the Hohenzollern family, rulers of Prussia and then Germany, once stood. The palace is a phantom sight, long gone, but its occupants were responsible for just about all you'll see. Alexanderplatz, which marks the end of this walk, is near the base of the giant TV Tower hovering in the distance.

• Pass all the way through the gate and stand in the middle of...

▲Pariser Platz

"Parisian Square," so named after the Prussians defeated Napoleon in 1813, was once filled with important government buildings—all bombed to smithereens in World War II. For decades, it was an unrecognizable, deserted no-man's-land—cut off from both East and West by the Wall. But now it's rebuilt, and the banks, hotels, and embassies that were here before the bombing have reclaimed their original places—with a few additions, including a palace of coffee: Starbucks. The winners of World War II enjoy this prime real estate: The American, French, British, and Soviet (now Russian) embassies are all on or near this square.

As you face the gate, to your right is the French Embassy, and to your left is the **US Embassy.** This reopened in its historic location in 2008. The building has been controversial: For safety's sake, Uncle Sam wanted more of a security zone around the building, but the Germans wanted to keep Pariser Platz a welcoming people zone. (Throughout the world, American embassies are the most fortified buildings in town.) The compromise: The extra security the US wanted is built into the structure. Easy-on-the-eyes barriers keep potential car bombs at a distance, and its front door is on the side farthest from the Brandenburg Gate.

Turn your back to the gate. On the right, jutting into the square, is the ritzy **Hotel Adlon**, long called home by visiting stars and VIPs. In its heyday, it hosted such notables as Charlie Chaplin, Albert Einstein, and Greta Garbo. It was the setting for Garbo's most famous line, "I vant to be alone," uttered in the film *Grand Hotel.* Damaged by the Russians just after World War II, the original hotel was closed with the construction of the nearby Wall in 1961 and later demolished. Today's grand Adlon was rebuilt in 1997. It was here that Michael Jackson shocked millions by dangling his baby, Blanket, over the railing (second balcony up).

• *Between the hotel and the US Embassy are two buildings worth a quick visit: the DZ Bank building (by Frank Gehry) and the glassy Academy of Arts. Enjoy the fun-loving scene on the square, and when you're ready to move on, work your way over to these two buildings; we'll enter both, then leave Pariser Platz through the Academy of Arts.*

DZ Bank Building: This building's architect, Frank Gehry, is famous for Bilbao's Guggenheim Museum, Prague's Dancing House, Seattle's Experience Music Project, Chicago's Millennium Park, and Los Angeles' Walt Disney Concert Hall. Gehry fans might be surprised at the bank building's low profile. Structures on Pariser Platz are designed so as not to draw attention away from the Brandenburg Gate. But to get your fix of wild and colorful Gehry, step into the lobby. Built in 2001 as an office complex and conference center, its undulating interior is like a big, slithery fish. Gehry explained, "The form of the fish is the best example of movement. I try to capture this movement in my buildings." For more of the architect's vision, read the nearby plaque.

• *Leaving the DZ Bank, turn right and head into the next building, the...*

Academy of Arts (Akademie der Künste): The glassy arcade is open daily (10:00-22:00, WC in basement, café serving light meals). Just past the café is the office where Albert Speer, Hitler's architect, planned the rebuilding of postwar Berlin into "Welthauptstadt Germania"—the grandiose "world capital" of Nazi Europe. Pass through the glass door to see Speer's favorite statue, *Prometheus* (c. 1900). This is the kind of art that turned Hitler on: a strong, soldierly, vital man, defending the homeland. Anticipating the bombs, Speer had the statue bricked up in the basement here where it lay, undiscovered, until 1995.

This building provides a handy and interesting passage to the Holocaust memorial on the other side.

• *Exit the building out the back. Across the street, to the right, stretches the vast Holocaust memorial. For orientation's sake, note that the small monument to homosexual victims of the Nazis is among the trees beyond the Holocaust monument (to the right). And Hitler's bunker, where he committed suicide, is straight ahead a block and a half (under a parking lot).*

Now, *focus on the sea of gray pillars before you.*

▲▲Memorial to the Murdered Jews of Europe (Denkmal für die Ermordeten Juden Europas)

This Holocaust memorial, consisting of 2,711 gravestone-like pillars (called "stelae") and completed in 2005, is an essential stop for

any visit to Berlin. It was the first formal, German government-sponsored Holocaust memorial. Using the word "murdered" in the title was intentional and a big deal. Germany, as a nation, was officially admitting to a crime. Jewish American architect Peter Eisenman won the competition for the commission.

Cost and Hours: The memorial is free and always open. The information center is open Tue-Sun 10:00-20:00, Oct-March until 19:00, closed Mon year-round; last entry 45 minutes before closing, S-Bahn: Brandenburger Tor or Potsdamer Platz, tel. 030/2639-4336, www.stiftung-denkmal.de. The €4 audioguide augments the experience.

Visiting the Memorial: The pillars, made of hollow concrete, stand in a gently sunken area, which can be entered from any side. The number of pillars isn't symbolic of anything; it's simply how many fit on the provided land. The pillars are all about the same size, but of differing heights. The memorial's location—where the Wall once stood—is coincidental. Nazi propagandist Joseph Goebbels' bunker was discovered during the work and left buried under the northeast corner of the memorial.

Once you enter the memorial, notice that people seem to appear and disappear between the columns, and that no matter where you are, the exit always seems to be up. The memorial is thoughtfully lit at night and guarded.

The monument was criticized for focusing on just one of the groups targeted by the Nazis, but the German government has now erected memorials to other victims. It's also been criticized because there's nothing intrinsically Jewish about it. Some were struck that there's no central gathering point or place for a ceremony. Like death, you enter it alone.

There is no one intended interpretation. Is it a symbolic cemetery, or an intentionally disorienting labyrinth? It's up to the visitor to derive the meaning, while pondering this horrible chapter in human history.

Memorial Information Center: The pondering takes place under the sky. For the learning, go under the field of concrete

pillars to the state-of-the-art information center. Inside, a thought-provoking exhibit (well-explained in English) studies the Nazi system of extermination and humanizes the victims, while also providing space for silent reflection. In the Starting Hall, exhibits trace the historical context of the Nazi and WWII era, while six portraits—representing the six million Jewish victims—look out on visitors. The Room of Dimensions has glowing boxes in the floor containing diaries, letters, and final farewells penned by Holocaust victims. The Room of Families presents case studies of 15 Jewish families from around Europe, to more fully convey the European Jewish experience. Remember: Behind these 15 stories are millions more tales of despair, tragedy, and survival. In the Room of Names, a continually running soundtrack lists the names and brief biographical sketches of Holocaust victims; reading the names of all those murdered would take more than six and a half years. The Room of Sites documents some 220 different places of genocide. You'll also find exhibits about other Holocaust monuments and memorials, a searchable database of victims, and a video archive of interviews with survivors.

• *Wander through the gray pillars, but eventually emerge on the corner with the Information Center. Cross Hannah-Arendt-Strasse and go a half block farther. Walk alongside the rough parking lot (left side of street) to the info plaque over the...*

Site of Hitler's Bunker

You're standing atop the buried remains of the *Führerbunker*. In early 1945, as Allied armies advanced on Berlin and Nazi Germany lay in ruins, Hitler and his staff retreated to a bunker complex behind the former Reich Chancellery. He stayed there for two months. It was here, as the Soviet army tightened its noose on the capital, that Hitler and Eva Braun, his wife of less than 48 hours, committed suicide on April 30, 1945. A week later, the war in Europe was over. The info board presents a detailed cutaway illustration of the bunker complex plus a timeline tracing its history and

Imagining Hitler in the 21st Century

More than six decades after the end of World War II, the bunker where Hitler killed himself lies hidden underneath a Berlin parking lot. While the Churchill War Rooms are a major sight in London, no one wants to turn Hitler's final stronghold into a tourist attraction.

Germans tread lightly on their past. It took 65 years for the Germany History Museum to organize its first exhibit on the life of Hitler. Even then, the exhibit was careful not to give neo-Nazis any excuse to celebrate—even the size of the Hitler portraits was kept to a minimum.

The image of Hitler has been changing in Germany. No longer is he exclusively an evil mass murderer; rather, sometimes he is portrayed as a nervous wreck, such as in the 2004 film *Downfall*, or as an object of derision. He's even a wax figure in the Berlin branch of Madame Tussauds.

But 21st-century Germans still treat the subject with extraordinary sensitivity. The Bavarian state government holds the copyright to Hitler's political manifesto—*Mein Kampf*—and won't allow any version to be published in German, even one annotated by historians (although it is readily available on the Internet and outside Germany). Any visit to Hitler's mountain retreat in Berchtesgaden includes a stop at the Nazi Documentation Center, where visitors see Nazi artifacts carefully placed in their historical context.

Many visitors to Berlin are curious about Hitler sites, but few artifacts of that dark period survive. The German Resistance Memorial is presented in German only and is difficult for the tourist to appreciate (though it has a helpful audioguide in English; see page 85). Hitler's bunker is completely erased from view, though the location is marked by a small information board. The best way to learn about Hitler sites is to take a Third Reich tour offered by one of the many local walking-tour companies (see "Tours in Berlin," page 15), or to visit the Topography of Terror, a fascinating exhibit located in a rebuilt hall on the same spot where the SS and Gestapo headquarters once stood (see page 63).

It's a balancing act, but when it comes to *der Führer*, Germans seem to be confronting their regrettable past.

ultimate fate (the roof was removed and the bunker filled with dirt, then covered over).

• *From here, you can visit the next memorial (which is important, but visually underwhelming and a bit of a detour), or you can continue the walk. To do either, first head back to Hannah-Arendt-Strasse. To rejoin the walk, turn right, go one block, then head up Wilhelmstrasse to Unter den Linden. To see the memorial, go left one block at Hannah-Arendt-*

Strasse, cross the street, and head down a path into Tiergarten park. There, look for a large, dark gray concrete box...

Memorial to the Homosexuals Persecuted Under the National Socialist Regime

There's no inscription or signage of any sort on this stark memorial—just a small window through which you can watch a black-and-white film loop of same-sex couples kissing. The message: Life and love are precious, regardless of who we are. The law against homosexuality in Germany had been on the books since 1850, and Hitler enforced it with brutality.

• *Now return to Unter den Linden by backtracking a couple of blocks down Hannah-Arendt-Strasse, then turning left on Wilhelmstrasse. Because Wilhelmstrasse was a main street of the German government during WWII, it was completely bombed and is new today. The pedestrianized part of the street is home to the British Embassy. The fun, purple color of its wall is the colors of the Union Jack mixed together.*

When you get back on Unter den Linden, stand in the median, in front of Hotel Adlon.

▲▲Unter den Linden

Unter den Linden is the heart of the former East Berlin. In the good old days, this was one of Europe's grand boulevards. In the

15th century, this carriageway led from the palace to the hunting grounds (today's big Tiergarten). In the 17th century, Hohenzollern princes and princesses moved in and built their palaces here so they could be near the Prussian king.

Named centuries ago for its thousands of linden trees, this was the most elegant street of Prussian Berlin before Hitler's time, and the main drag of East Berlin after his reign. Hitler replaced the venerable trees—many 250 years old—with Nazi flags. Popular discontent drove him to replant the trees.

Today, Unter den Linden is no longer a depressing Cold War cul-de-sac, and its pre-Hitler strolling café ambience has returned. It is divided, roughly at Friedrichstrasse, into a business section, which stretches toward the Brandenburg Gate, and a cultural section, which spreads out toward Alexanderplatz. Frederick the Great wanted to have culture, mainly the opera and the university, closer to his palace and to keep business (read: banks) farther away, near the city walls.

• *Begin walking toward the giant TV Tower. In front of Hotel Adlon is the Brandenburger Tor S-Bahn station. Cover a bit of Unter den Linden underground by climbing down its steps and walking along the platform.*

Ghost Subway Station: The Brandenburger Tor S-Bahn station is one of Berlin's former ghost subway stations. During the Cold War, most underground train tunnels were simply blocked at the border. But a few Western lines looped through the East and then back into the West. To make a little hard Western cash, the Eastern government rented the use of these tracks to the West, but all but one of the stations in East Berlin were strictly off-limits. For 28 years, these stations were unused, as Western trains slowly passed through and passengers saw only eerie DDR (East German) guards and lots of cobwebs. Literally within days of the fall of the Wall, these stations were reopened, and today they are a time warp, looking much as they did when built in 1931, with dreary old green tiles and original signage on ticket kiosks.

• *Walk along the track (the walls are lined with historic photos of the Reichstag through the ages) and exit on the other side. You'll pop out at the Russian Embassy's front yard. Belly up to the bars and look in.*

Russian Embassy: This was the first big postwar building project in East Berlin. It's built in the powerful, simplified Neoclassical style that Stalin liked. While not as important now as it was a few years ago, it's as immense as ever. It flies the Russian white, blue, and red. Find the hammer-and-sickle motif decorating the window frames—a reminder of the days when Russia was the USSR.

• *At the next intersection (Glinkastrasse), cross to the other side of Unter den Linden. At #40 is the entertaining...*

Berlin Story Bookstore and Museum: Berlin Story is two shops side by side (on the left are Cold War souvenirs and the museum; on the right, the bookstore). The bookshop has just about the best range anywhere of English-language titles on Berlin (Mon-Sat 10:00-19:00, Sun 10:00-18:00). They have also created a beefy little museum covering the main points of modern Berlin history and a video about the Wall. It offers a vivid swing through the tumultuous story of this city (€5, or €4 with this book, includes good audioguide, daily 10:00-20:00, until 19:00 in Jan-Feb).

• *A few steps farther down is the...*

Intersection of Unter den Linden and Friedrichstrasse: This is perhaps the most central crossroads in Berlin. And for several years, it will be a mess as Berlin builds a new connection in its already extensive subway system. All over Berlin, you'll see big, colorful **water pipes** running aboveground. Wherever there are big construction projects, streets are laced with these drainage pipes. Berlin's high water table means that any new basement comes with lots of pumping out.

Looking at the jaunty DDR-style pedestrian lights at this intersection is a reminder that very little of the old East survives. Construction has been a theme since the Wall came down. The West lost no time in consuming the East; consequently, some have felt a wave of *Ost*-**algia** for the old days of East Berlin. At election time, a surprising number of formerly East Berlin voters still opt for the extreme left party, which has ties to the bygone Communist Party—although the East-West divide is no longer at the forefront of most voters' minds.

One symbol of that communist era has been given a reprieve: the DDR-style pedestrian lights you'll see along Unter den Linden (and throughout much of Berlin). The perky red and green men—called *Ampelmännchen*—were recently threatened with replacement by far less jaunty Western-style signs. But, after a 10-year court battle, the wildly popular DDR signals were kept after all.

When the little green *Ampelmännchen* says you can go, cross Unter den Linden to the **VW Automobil Forum,** which shows off the latest models from the many car companies owned by VW—like Bentley and Bugatti (Mon-Fri 10:00-20:00, closed Sat-Sun, enter on Friedrichstrasse, WC in basement).

• *Before continuing down Unter den Linden, look farther down...*

Friedrichstrasse: Before the war, this zone was the heart of Berlin. In the 1920s, Berlin was famous for its anything-goes love of life. This was the cabaret drag, a springboard to stardom for young and vampy entertainers like Marlene Dietrich. (Born in 1901, Dietrich starred in the first major German talkie—*The Blue Angel*—and then headed straight to Hollywood.) Over the last few years, this boulevard—lined with super-department stores (such as Galeries Lafayette) and big-time hotels (such as the Hilton and Regent)—is attempting to replace Ku'damm as the grand commerce-and-café boulevard of Berlin. More recently, western Berlin is retaliating with some new stores of its own. And so far, Friedrichstrasse gets little more than half the pedestrian traffic that Ku'damm gets in the West. Why? Locals complain that this area has no daily life—no supermarkets, not much ethnic street food, and so on.

Consider detouring to Galeries Lafayette, with its cool marble-and-glass, waste-of-space interior (Mon-Sat 10:00-20:00, closed Sun; check out the vertical garden on its front wall, belly up to its amazing ground-floor viewpoint, or have lunch in its recommended basement food court).

• *If you continued down Friedrichstrasse, you'd wind up at the sights listed under "South of Unter den Linden"—including Checkpoint Charlie (a 10-minute walk from here).*

But we'll head down Unter den Linden a few more blocks, past the large equestrian statue of Frederick the Great, and turn right into the square called Bebelplatz. Stand on the glass window set into the pavement in the center.

Bebelplatz

Prussia, likened to a modern-day Sparta, was all about its military. Voltaire famously said, "Whereas some states have an army, the Prussian army has a state." But Frederick the Great—who ruled from 1740 to 1786—established Prussia not just as a military power, but also as a cultural and intellectual heavyweight. This square was the center of the cultural capital that Frederick envisioned. His grand palace was just down the street (explained later).

Imagine that it's 1760. Pan around the square to see Frederick's contributions to Prussian culture. Everything is draped with Greek-inspired Prussian pomp. Sure, Prussia was a modern-day Sparta. But Frederick also built an **"Athens on the Spree"**—an enlightened and cultured society.

To visually survey the square, start with the university across the street and spin counterclockwise:

Humboldt University, across Unter den Linden, is one of Europe's greatest. Marx and Lenin (not the brothers or the sisters) studied here, as did the Grimms (both brothers) and more than two dozen Nobel Prize winners. Einstein, who was Jewish, taught here until taking a spot at Princeton in 1932 (smart guy). Used-book merchants set up their tables in front of the university.

Turn 90 degrees to the left. The former **state library** (labeled *Juristische Fakultät*) is where Vladimir Lenin studied law during much of his exile from Russia. Bombed in WWII, the library was rebuilt in the original style only because Lenin studied here. If you climb to the second floor of the library and go through the door opposite the stairs, you'll see a 1968 vintage stained-glass window depicting Lenin's life's work with almost biblical reverence. On the ground floor is Tim's Espressobar, a great little café with light food, student prices, and garden seating (€3 plates, Mon-Fri 8:00-20:00, Sat 9:00-17:00, closed Sun, handy WC).

Next to the library, the square is closed by one of Berlin's swankiest lodgings—**Hotel de Rome,** housed in a historic bank building with a spa and lap pool fitted into the former vault.

The round, Catholic **St. Hedwig's Church,** nicknamed the "upside-down teacup," is a statement of religious and cultural tolerance. The pragmatic Frederick the Great wanted to encourage the integration of Catholic Silesians after his empire annexed their region in 1742, and so the first Catholic church since the Reformation was built in Berlin. (St. Hedwig is the patron saint of Silesia, a region now shared by Germany, Poland, and the Czech Republic.) Like all Catholic churches in Berlin, St. Hedwig's is not on the street, but stuck in a kind of back lot—indicating inferiority to Protestant churches. You can step inside the church to see the cheesy DDR government renovation (generally daily until 17:00).

The **German State Opera** was bombed in 1941, rebuilt to bolster morale and to celebrate its centennial in 1943, and bombed again in 1945. It's currently undergoing an extensive renovation.

Now look down through the glass you're standing on: The room of empty bookshelves is a memorial repudiating the notorious Nazi **book burning.** It was on this square in 1933 that staff and students from the university threw 20,000 newly forbidden books (authored by Einstein, Hemmingway, Freud, and T.S. Elliot, among others) into a huge bonfire on the orders of the Nazi propaganda minister, Joseph Goebbels. In fact, Goebbels himself tossed books onto the fire, condemning writers to the flames. He declared, "The era of extreme Jewish intellectualism has come to an end, and the German revolution has again opened the way for the true essence of being German."

The Prussian heritage of Frederick the Great was one of culture and enlightenment. Hitler chose this square to thoroughly squash those ideals, dramatically signaling that the era of tolerance and openness was over. Hitler was establishing a new age of intolerance where German-ness was correct and diversity was evil.

A plaque nearby reminds us of the prophetic quote by the German poet Heinrich Heine. In 1820, he wrote, "Where they burn books, in the end they will also burn people." The Nazis despised Heine because he was a Jew who converted to Christianity. A century later, his books were among those that went up in flames on this spot.

This monument reminds us of that chilling event in 1933, while also inspiring vigilance against the anti-intellectual, scaremongering forces of today that would burn the thoughts of people they fear to defend their culture from diversity.

• Cross Unter den Linden to the university side. Just past the university is a Greek-temple-like building set in the small chestnut-tree-filled park. This is the...

Neue Wache

This is the emperor's "New Guardhouse" (Neue Wache), from 1816. Converted by communist authorities in 1960 to a memorial to the victims of fascism, the structure was transformed again, after the Wall fell, into a national memorial. Look inside, where a replica of the Käthe Kollwitz statue, *Mother with Her Dead Son,* is surrounded by thought-provoking silence. It marks the tombs of Germany's unknown soldier and an unknown concentration camp victim. The inscription in front reads, "To the victims of war and tyranny." Read the entire statement in English (on wall, left of entrance). The memorial, open to the sky, incorporates the elements—sunshine, rain, snow—falling on this modern-day *pietà.*

*• After the Neue Wache, the next building you'll see is Berlin's pink-yet-formidable Zeughaus (arsenal). Dating from 1695, it's considered the oldest building on the boulevard, and now houses the excellent **German History Museum**—well worth a visit.*

Continuing down Unter den Linden, you'll cross a bridge to reach...

Museum Island (Museumsinsel)

This island is filled with some of Berlin's most impressive museums (all part of the Staatliche Museen zu Berlin). The earliest building—the Altes Museum—

went up in the 1820s, and the rest of the complex began taking shape in the 1840s under King Friedrich Wilhelm IV, who envisioned the island as an oasis of culture and learning. The island's imposing Neoclassical buildings host five grand museums: the **Pergamon Museum** (classical antiquities, including the top-notch Pergamon Altar, with its temple and frieze; this is undergoing restoration—expect partial closures for the next few years); the **Neues Museum** ("New Museum," famous for its Egyptian collection with the bust of Queen Nefertiti); the **Old National Gallery** (Alte Nationalgalerie, 19th-century art, mostly German Romantic and Realist paintings); the **Altes Mu-**

seum ("Old Museum," more antiquities); and the **Bode Museum** (European statuary and paintings through the ages, coins, and Byzantine art).

• *For now, we'll continue on our walk. Before leaving Museum Island, check out a few of its other landmarks. First is the big, inviting park in the middle of the island, called the...*

Lustgarten

For 300 years, the island's big central square has flip-flopped between being a military parade ground and a people-friendly park, depending upon the political tenor of the time. During the revolutions of 1848, the Kaiser's troops dispersed a protesting crowd that had assembled here, sending demonstrators onto footpaths. Karl Marx later commented, "It is impossible to have a revolution in a country where people stay off the grass."

Hitler enjoyed giving speeches from the top of the museum steps overlooking this square. In fact, he had the square landscaped to fit his symmetrical tastes and propaganda needs.

In 1999, the Lustgarten was made into a park (read the history posted in the corner opposite the church). On a sunny day, it's packed with relaxing locals and is one of Berlin's most enjoyable public spaces.

• *The huge church on Museum Island is the...*

Berlin Cathedral (Berliner Dom)

This century-old church's bombastic Wilhelmian architecture is a Protestant assertion of strength. It seems to proclaim, "A mighty fortress is our God." The years of Kaiser Wilhelm's rule, from 1888 to 1918, were a busy age of building. Germany had recently been united (1871), and the emperor wanted to give his capital stature and legitimacy. Wilhelm's buildings are over-the-top statements: Neoclassical, Neo-Baroque, and Neo-Renaissance, with stucco and gold-tiled mosaics. This cathedral, while Protestant, is as ornate as if it were Catholic. With the emperor's lead, this ornate style came into vogue, and anyone who wanted to be associated with the royal class built this way. (Aside from the cathedral, the other big examples of Wilhelmian architecture in Berlin are the Reichstag—which we saw earlier—and the Kaiser Wilhelm Memorial Church.) The church is most impressive from the outside, and there's no way to even peek inside without a pricey ticket.

Cost and Hours: €7 includes access to dome gallery, €10 with audioguide, not covered by Museum Island or Museumspass ticket, discount with WelcomeCard, Mon-Sat 9:00-20:00, Sun 12:00-20:00, until 19:00 Oct-March, closes early—around 17:30—on some days for concerts, interior closed but dome open during services, tel. 030/2026-9136, www.berliner-dom.de. The cathedral hosts many organ concerts (often on weekends, tickets from about €10 always available at the door).

Visiting the Church: Inside, the great reformers (Luther, Calvin, and company) stand around the brilliantly restored dome like stern saints guarding their theology. Frederick I rests in an ornate tomb (right transept, near entrance to dome). The 270-step climb to the outdoor dome gallery is tough but offers pleasant, breezy views of the city at the finish line. The crypt downstairs is not worth a look.

• *Kitty-corner across Unter den Linden from the Berlin Cathedral is a huge construction site, known as...*

Humboldt-Forum

For centuries, this was the site of the Baroque palace of the Hohenzollern dynasty of Brandenburg and Prussia. Much of that palace actually survived World War II but was replaced by the communists with a blocky, Soviet-style "Palace" of the Republic—East Berlin's parliament building/entertainment complex and a showy symbol of the communist days. The landmark building fell into disrepair after reunification, and by 2009 had been dismantled.

After much debate about how to use this prime real estate, the German parliament decided to construct the Humboldt-Forum, a huge public venue filled with museums, shops, galleries, and concert halls behind a facade constructed in imitation of the original Hohenzollern palace. With a €1.2 billion price tag, many Berliners consider the reconstruction plan a complete waste of money. Funding disappointments are delaying the project and confusing the public. The mayor recently declared that it should be finished by 2019.

In the meantime, the temporary **Humboldt-Box** has been set up. Until it gets in the way and has to be demolished, it will help the public follow the construction of the Humboldt-Forum. The multiple floors of the futuristic "box" display building plans and models for the project and some otherwise dry exhibits. The real draw here is the view from the top and a fabulous model of Berlin (€4, discount with Museumspass and WelcomeCard, daily 10:00-20:00, after that, free entry to terrace-café until 23:00, tel. 01805-030-707, www.humboldt-box.com). On the top floor, the terrace-café with unobstructed views over Berlin serves coffee, desserts, and light food until 18:00, and a dinner menu after that (€8-13 lunch dishes, €15-22 dinners).

• *Head to the bridge just beyond the Berlin Cathedral, with views of the riverbank. Consider...*

Strolling and Cruising the Spree River

With the reunification of Berlin, the Spree River has become people-friendly and welcoming. A park-like trail leads from the Berlin Cathedral to the Hauptbahnhof, with impromptu "beach-side" beer gardens with imported sand, BBQs in pocket parks, and lots of locals walking their dogs, taking a lazy bike ride, or jogging.

You may notice "don't drop anchor" signs. There are still un-exploded WWII bombs around town, and many are in this river. Every month, several bombs are found at construction sites. Their triggers were set for the hard ground of Scotland testing grounds, and because Berlin sits upon soft soil (the name of the city likely comes from an old word for "swamp"), an estimated one of every ten bombs didn't explode.

The recommended **Spree River boat tours** depart from the riverbank near the bridge by the Berlin Cathedral.

• *Before crossing the bridge (and leaving Museum Island), look down the river in the distance. To the right, the pointy twin spires of the 13th-century Nikolai Church mark the center of medieval Berlin. This **Nikolaiviertel** (Viertel means "quarter") was restored by the DDR and trendy in the last years of communism. To the left is the gilded **New Synagogue** dome, rebuilt after WWII bombing.*

Now look down along the riverbank (directly across from the back-side of the Berlin Cathedral), for the...

▲DDR Museum

The exhibits here offer an interesting look at life in the former East Germany (DDR) without the negative spin most museums give. It's well-stocked with kitschy everyday items from the communist period, plus photos, video clips, and concise English explanations. The exhibits are interactive—you're encouraged to pick up and handle anything that isn't behind glass.

Cost and Hours: €6, not covered by Museumspass, discount with WelcomeCard, daily 10:00-20:00, Sat until 22:00, just across the Spree from Museum Island at Karl-Liebknecht-Strasse 1, tel. 030/847-123-731, www.ddr-museum.de.

Visiting the Museum: You'll crawl through a Trabant car (designed by East German engineers to compete with the West's popular VW Beetle) and pick up some DDR-era jokes ("East Germany had 39 newspapers, four radio stations, two TV chan-nels...and one opinion.") The reconstructed communist-era home lets you tour the kitchen, living room, bedrooms, and more. You'll learn about the Russian-imported *Dacha*—the simple countryside cottage (owned by one in six East Germans) used for weekend retreats from the grimy city. (Others vacationed on the Baltic Coast, where nudism was all the rage, as a very revealing display explains.) Lounge in DDR cinema chairs as you view a subtitled propaganda film or clips from beloved-in-the-East TV shows (including the popular kids' show *Sandmännchen*—"Little Sandman"). Even the meals served in the attached restaurant are based on DDR-era recipes.

• *From the bridge, continue walking straight toward the TV Tower, down the big boulevard, which here changes its name to...*

Karl-Liebknecht-Strasse

The first big building on the left after the bridge is the **SAS Radisson Hotel** and shopping center, with a huge aquarium in the center. The elevator goes right through the middle of a deep-sea world. (You can see it from the unforgettable Radisson hotel lobby—tuck in your shirt and walk past the guards with the confidence of a guest who's sleeping there.) It's a huge glass cylinder rising high above the central bar (best seen from the left corner as you enter). Here in the center of the old communist capital, it seems that capitalism has settled in with a spirited vengeance.

In the park immediately across the street (a big jaywalk from the Radisson) are grandfatherly statues of **Marx** and **Engels** (nick-named the "old pensioners"). Surrounding them are stainless-steel monoliths with evocative photos illustrating the struggles of the workers of the world.

Farther along, where Karl-Liebknecht-Strasse intersects with Spandauer Strasse, look right to see the red-brick **city hall**. It was built after the revolutions of 1848 and arguably the first democratic building in the city.

Continue toward **Marien Church** (from 1270), with its spire mirroring the TV Tower. An artist's rendering helps you follow the interesting but very faded old "Dance of Death" mural that wraps around the narthex inside the door.

• *Immediately across the street from the church, detour a half-block down little Rosenstrasse to find a beautiful memorial set in a park.*

Women's Protest Memorial: This is a reminder of a success-ful and courageous protest against Nazi policies. In 1943, when "privileged Jews" (men married to Gentile women) were arrested, their wives demonstrated en masse on this street, home to Berlin's oldest synagogue (now gone). They actually won the freedom of their men. Note the Berliner on the bench nearby. As most Ber-liners did, he looks the other way, even when these courageous women demonstrated that you could speak up and be heard under the Nazis.

• *Back on Karl-Liebknecht-Strasse, look up at the 1,200-foot-tall...*

TV Tower (Fernsehturm): Built (with Swedish know-how) in 1969 for the 20th anniversary of the communist government, the tower was meant to show the power of the atheistic state at a time when DDR leaders were having the crosses removed from church domes and spires. But when the sun hit the tower—the greatest spire in East Berlin—a huge cross was reflected on the mirrored ball. Cynics called it "God's Revenge." East Berliners dubbed the tower the "Tele-Asparagus." They joked that if it fell over, they'd have an elevator to the West.

The tower has a fine view from halfway up, offering a handy city orientation and an interesting look at the flat, red-roofed sprawl of Berlin—including a peek inside the city's many courtyards, called *Höfe* (€12.50, daily March-Oct 9:00-24:00, Nov-Feb 10:00-24:00, www.tv-turm.de). The retro tower is quite trendy these days, so it can be crowded (your ticket comes with an assigned entry time). Consider a kitschy trip to the observation deck for the view and lunch in its revolving restaurant (mediocre food, €12 plates, horrible lounge music, reservations smart for dinner, tel. 030/242-3333, www.tv-turm.de).

• *Walk four more minutes down the boulevard past the TV Tower and toward the big railway overpass. Just before the bridge, on the left, is the half-price ticket booth called* **Hekticket**—*stop in to see what's on.*

Walk under the train bridge and continue for a long half-block (passing the Galeria Kaufhof mall). Turn right onto a broad pedestrian street, and go through the low tunnel into the big square where blue U-Bahn station signs mark...

Alexanderplatz

This square was the commercial pride and joy of East Berlin. The Kaufhof department store (now Galeria Kaufhof) was the ultimate

shopping mecca for Easterners. It, along with the two big surviving 1920s "functionalist" buildings, defined the square. Alexanderplatz is still a landmark, with a major U-Bahn/S-Bahn station. The once-futuristic, now-retro "World Time Clock," installed in 1969, is a nostalgic favorite and remains a popular meeting point.

Stop in the square for a coffee and to people-watch. You may see the dueling human hot-dog stands. These hot-dog hawkers wear ingenious harnesses that let them cook and sell tasty, cheap German sausages on the fly. (Grillwalker is the original company; Grillrunner is the copycat.) While the square can get a little rough at night, it's generally a great scene.

• *Our orientation stroll is finished. From here, you can hike back a bit to catch the riverboat tour or visit Museum Island or the German History museums, take in the sights south of Unter den Linden, venture into the colorful Prenzlauer Berg neighborhood, or consider extending this foray into eastern Berlin by way of Karl-Marx-Allee. These options are covered in detail in the next section.*

Sights in Eastern Berlin

Many of Berlin's top sights and landmarks (including **Brandenburg Gate**, the **Memorial to the Murdered Jews of Europe**, **Pariser Platz, Unter den Linden,** and **Alexanderplatz**) are described in detail in the self-guided walk (see above). Additional sights mentioned in passing along that walk (including the **Reichstag**, **German History Museum,** and the museums of **Museum Island**)—as well as other points of interest in the eastern part of Berlin—are detailed below.

▲▲Reichstag

Germany's historic parliament building—completed in 1894, burned in 1933, sad and lonely in a no-man's land throughout the Cold War, and finally rebuilt and topped with a glittering glass cupola in 1999—is a symbol of a proudly reunited nation. Its exterior and history are stirring, and it's fascinating to climb up the twin ramps that spiral through its dome. Because of security concerns, getting in requires a reservation.

Cost and Hours: Free, but reservations required—see below, daily 8:00-24:00, last entry at 22:00, metal detectors, no big luggage allowed, Platz der Republik 1; S- or U-Bahn: Friedrichstrasse, Brandenburger Tor, or Bundestag; tel. 030/2273-2152, www.bundestag.de.

Reservations: To visit the dome, you'll need to **reserve online** (free); spots book up several days in advance. Go to www.bundestag.de, click "English" and—from the "Visit the Bundestag" menu—select "Online registration." On this page, select "Visit the dome" to choose your preferred date and time (you can request up to three different time slots). You'll be sent an email link to a website where you'll enter details for each person in your party. After completing this form, another email will confirm your request, and a final email will contain your reservation (with a letter you must print out and bring with you).

If you're in Berlin without a reservation, try dropping by the tiny visitors center on the Tiergarten side of Scheidemannstrasse, across from Platz der Republik (open daily 8:00-20:00; go between

8:00-10:00 to avoid lines; you must book no less than 2 hours and no more than 2 days out; when booking, the whole party must be present and ID is required).

Getting In: Report a few minutes before your appointed time to the temporary-looking entrance facility in front of the Reichstag, and be ready to show ID and your reservation print-out. After passing through an airport-like security check, you'll wait with other visitors for a guard to take you to the Reichstag entrance.

Tours: Pick up the English **"Outlooks" flier** when you exit the elevator at the top of the Reichstag. The free GPS-driven **audioguide** explains the building and narrates the view as you wind up the spiral ramp to the top of the dome; the commentary starts automatically as you step onto the bottom of the ramp.

❍ Self-Guided Tour: The open, airy lobby towers 100 feet high, with 65-foot-tall colors of the German flag. See-through glass doors show the **central legislative chamber.** The message: There will be no secrets in this government. Look inside. Spreading his wings behind the podium is a stylized German eagle, the *Bundestagsadler* (a.k.a. the "fat hen"), representing the Bundestag (each branch of government has its own symbolic eagle). Notice the doors marked *Ja* (Yes), *Nein* (No), and *Enthalten* (Abstain)... an homage to the Bundestag's traditional "sheep jump" way of counting votes by exiting the chamber through the corresponding door (for critical votes, however, all 669 members vote with electronic cards).

Ride the elevator to the base of the glass **dome.** Pick up the free audioguide and take some time to study the photos and read

the circle of captions (around the base of the central funnel) for an excellent exhibit telling the Reichstag story. Then study the surrounding architecture: a broken collage of new on old, torn between antiquity and modernity, like Germany's history. Notice the dome's giant and unobtrusive sunscreen that moves as necessary with the sun. Peer down through the skylight to look over the shoulders of the elected representatives at work. For Germans, the best view from here is down—keeping a close eye on their government.

Start at the ramp nearest the elevator and wind up to the top of the **double ramp.** Take a 360-degree survey of the city as you hike: The big park is the **Tiergarten,** the "green lungs of Berlin." Beyond

that is the **Teufelsberg** ("Devil's Hill"). Built of rubble from the destroyed city in the late 1940s, it was famous during the Cold War as a powerful ear of the West—notice the telecommunications tower on top. Knowing the bombed-out and bulldozed story of their city, locals say, "You have to be suspicious when you see the nice, green park."

Find the **Victory Column** (Siegessäule), glimmering in the middle of the park. Hitler moved it in the 1930s from in front of the Reichstag to its present position in the Tiergarten as part of his grandiose vision for postwar Berlin. Next, scenes of the new Berlin spiral into view—**Potsdamer Platz,** marked by the conical glass tower that houses Sony's European headquarters. Continue circling left, and find the green chariot atop the **Brandenburg Gate.** Just to its left is the curving fish-like roof of the **DZ Bank** building, designed by the unconventional American architect Frank Gehry. The **Memorial to the Murdered Jews of Europe** stretches south of the Brandenburg Gate. Next, you'll see **former East Berlin** and the city's next huge construction zone, with a forest of 300-foot-tall skyscrapers in the works. Notice the **TV Tower,** the **Berlin Cathedral**'s massive dome, and the golden dome of the **New Synagogue.**

Follow the train tracks in the distance to the left toward Berlin's huge main train station, the **Hauptbahnhof.** Complete your spin-tour with the blocky, postmodern **Chancellery,** the federal government's headquarters. Continue spiraling up. You'll pass all the same sights again, twice, from a higher vantage point.

▲▲▲German History Museum (Deutsches Historisches Museum)

This fantastic museum is a two-part affair: the pink former Prussian arsenal building and the I. M. Pei-designed annex. The main building (fronting Unter den Linden) houses the permanent collection, offering the best look at German history under one roof, anywhere. The modern annex features good temporary exhibits surrounded by the work of a great contemporary architect. While this city has more than its share of hokey "museums" that slap together WWII and Cold War bric-a-brac, then charge too much for admission, this thoughtfully presented museum—with more than 8,000 artifacts telling not just the story of Berlin, but of all Germany—is clearly the top history museum in town.

Cost and Hours: €8, discount with WelcomeCard, daily 10:00-18:00, Unter den Linden 2, tel. 030/2030-4751, www.dhm. de.

Audioguide: For the most informative visit, invest in the excellent €3 audioguide, with six hours of info to choose from.

Visiting the Museum: The permanent collection packs two

huge rectangular floors of the old arsenal building with historical objects, photographs, and models—all well-described in English and intermingled with multimedia stations to help put everything in context. From the lobby, head upstairs to the **first floor** and work your way chronologically down. This floor traces German history from 1 B.C. to 1918, with exhibits on early cultures, the Middle Ages, Reformation, Thirty Years' War, German Empire, and World War I. You'll see a Roman floor mosaic, lots of models of higgledy-piggledy medieval towns and castles, tapestries, suits of armor, busts of great Germans, a Turkish tent from the Ottoman siege of Vienna (1683), flags from German unification in 1871 (the first time "Germany" existed as a nation), exhibits on everyday life in the tenements of the Industrial Revolution, and much more.

History marches on through the 20th century on the **ground floor,** including the Weimar Republic, Nazism, World War II, Allied occupation, and a divided Germany. Propaganda posters trumpet Germany's would-be post-WWI savior, Adolf Hitler. Look for the model of the impossibly huge, 950-foot-high, 180,000-capacity domed hall Hitler wanted to erect in the heart of Berlin, which he planned to re-envision as Welthauptstadt Germania, the "world capital" of his far-reaching Third Reich. Another model shows the sobering reality of Hitler's grandiosity: a crematorium at Auschwitz-Birkenau concentration camp in occupied Poland. The exhibit wraps up with chunks of the Berlin Wall, reunification, and a quick look at Germany today.

For architecture buffs, the big attraction is the **Pei annex** behind the history museum, which complements the museum with often-fascinating temporary exhibits. From the old building, cross through the courtyard (with the Pei glass canopy overhead) to reach the annex. A striking glassed-in spiral staircase unites four floors with surprising views and lots of light. It's here that you'll experience why Pei—famous for his glass pyramid at Paris' Louvre—is called the "perfector of classical modernism," "master of light," and a magician of uniting historical buildings with new ones. (If the museum is closed, or you don't have a ticket, venture down the street to the left of the museum—called Hinter dem Giesshaus—to see the Pei annex from the outside.)

Museum Island (Museumsinsel)

Some of Berlin's top museums are concentrated on this aptly named, centrally located island, just up Unter den Linden from the Brandenburg Gate. For specifics on each individual museum, read on.

Museum Island

A formidable renovation is under way on Museum Island. It seems Berlin was inspired by (and perhaps jealous of) the Louvre Pyramid entry in Paris and is building something to match: a single, grand, glass entry for the entire ensemble of museums on the island. When complete (it's hoped in 2019), a unified visitors center—the James-Simon-Galerie—will serve the island's five venerable but separate museums; the Pergamon Museum will get a fourth wing; tunnels will lace the complex together; and this will become one of the grandest museum zones in Europe (go to www.museum-sinsel-berlin.de for a look at the master plan). In the meantime, pardon their dust.

Cost: The €18 Museum Island Pass combo-ticket—covering all five museums—is a far better value than buying individual entries ranging from €10 to €14. All five museums are also included in the city's €24 Museums-spass. Special exhibits are extra.

Hours: The museums are open daily 10:00-18:00, with later hours on Thursday (until 20:00); the Old National Gallery is closed Monday.

When to Go: The busiest times are Saturday and Sunday mornings; the least-crowded time is Thursday evening, when the museums are open late.

Crowd-Beating Tips: Long ticket-buying lines plague the Pergamon Museum. Avoid them by purchasing your museum pass at one of the island's three never-crowded museums: Altes, Bode, or Old National Gallery. (From Unter den Linden, Altes is most convenient; if coming from Prenzlauer Berg, try the Bode.) You can also buy tickets online (www.smb.museum).

Getting There: The nearest S-Bahn station is Hackescher Markt, about a 10-minute walk away. From hotels in the Prenzlauer Berg, ride tram #M-1 to the end of line, and you're right at the Pergamon Museum.

Information: Tel. 030/266-424-242, www.smb.museum.

Eating Nearby: For lunch in the neighborhood, follow the elevated train tracks away from the Pergamon down Georgenstrasse.

Just for Fun: Germany's formidable leader, Angela Merkel, could live in the expansive digs at the Chancellery. But her husband (who's a professor here) and she have long lived in an apartment overlooking Museum Island. You'll see a couple of policemen providing modest protection in front of her place on Am Kupfergraben, directly across the bridge from the Pergamon Museum.

▲▲▲Pergamon Museum (Pergamonmuseum)

The star attraction of this world-class museum, part of Berlin's Collection of Classical Antiquities (Antikensammlung), is the

fantastic and gigantic Pergamon Altar. The Babylonian Ishtar Gate (slathered with glazed blue tiles from the 6th century B.C.) and the museum's ancient Greek, Mesopotamian, Roman, and early Islamic treasures are also impressive. But be warned: Closures and changes to exhibits will occur in stages over the next decade during a major renovation project, which will include building a fourth wing. The most notable closure will keep the Pergamon Altar off-view from the fall of 2014 until 2019. The north wing is already closed (its Greek and Roman sculptures, plus some vases and bronze figurines, can be seen at the Altes Museum; the north wing's Hellenistic architecture and artworks, however, won't be seen again until 2019).

Audioguide: Make ample use of the superb audioguide (included with admission)—it will broaden your experience. Punching #10 on the audioguide gets you the "Pergamon in 30 Minutes" general tour. Or follow my more succinct self-guided tour.

◐ **Self-Guided Tour:** With your museum pass, walk boldly by the long line of people who don't have or read guidebooks, and go directly in.

There's a lot to see in this museum (everything is well-described by posted English information and the included audioguide). The best plan for the casual visitor is to focus on a few highlights.

From the entrance, walk straight ahead to find the museum's namesake, the **Pergamon Altar.** Actually a 65-foot-wide temple, this "altar" comes from the second-century B.C. Greek city of Pergamon (near the west coast of today's Turkey). The Pergamon Altar was just one component of a spectacular hilltop ensemble—temples, sanctuaries, palaces, theaters, and other buildings erected to honor the gods—modeled after the Acropolis in Athens. (See a model of the complete Pergamon Acropolis to the right, as you face the stairs.)

Pergamon was excavated from 1878 to 1886 by German archaeologist Carl Humann, who unearthed fragments of the temple's frieze all over the site (many pieces had been "recycled" as building materials in later structures). The bits and pieces were brought here to Berlin, reassembled on this replica of the temple, and put on display in this purpose-built museum in 1930.

The temple replica re-creates the western third of the original building. Stairs lead up to a chamber with a small sacrificial altar, where priests and priestesses sacrificed and burned animals, while toga-clad Greeks assembled in awe at the foot of the stairs below.

Surviving pieces of a 269-foot-long frieze that wrapped around the entire temple dramatically spill onto the stairs and

around the room. Called the **Gigantomachy Frieze,** it shows the Greek gods under Zeus and Athena defeating the giants in a dramatic pig pile of mythological mayhem. Imagine how much more evocative these sculptures once were, slathered in colorful paint, gold, and silver trim.

So what's the fight about? Long before the time of man, an epic struggle pitted the titans against the gods. When the gods won, they thrust their foes into a miserable underworld (the mythological equivalent of purgatory) and settled in for a comfy period of rule atop Mount Olympus. But the troublesome race of giants—children of the earth goddess Gaia, mother of the titans—sought revenge. The giants had legs of slithering snakes that kept them in contact with the ground, allowing Gaia to make them immortal. This frieze captures a pivotal event, when the giants Alkyoneus and Porphyrion led a rebellion of their race against the gods. (The people of Pergamon appreciated the parallels between this story and their own noble struggle against unenlightened barbarians.)

With your back to the altar steps, look at the right end of the frieze to find panels with Zeus and Athena, locked in combat with the giants. Faint surviving labels on the cornice above the statues—in Greek, of course—help identify the combatants; the modern English letters below may prove more helpful.

Find the **Athena** panel. Athena (faceless, in the center, with the shield) and Nike (all that's left are her wings, right arm, and left leg) pull the chief giant Alkyoneus (his snake legs curling

around his bicep) up by his hair—breaking his connection to the earth, the source of his immortality. Below them, Gaia—the mother of the giants—rises up from her subterranean realm to lend a hand. (See the fear in Gaia's and Alkyoneus' tortured eyes.) Alkyoneus would survive this brush with Athena, only to be killed soon after by Hercules. (The statue of Hercules is missing—all that survives is one pathetic paw of his lion pelt.)

The **Zeus** panel to the left shows the (headless) king of the gods raining lightning bolts down on his enemies—including the snake-legged Porphyrion, with his back(side) toward us. Notice Zeus' disembodied right hand

up above, ready to pitch some serious heat. Fans of Greek mythology can take a slow walk along the entire length of the frieze, identifying their favorite gods and giants...the gang's all here. Before long, the giants will be history, and the gods can go back about their usual business of conspiring against each other and impregnating mortals.

Now turn left, cross the room, and go through the door on the far side. From Pergamon, flash-forward 300 years (and travel south 110 miles) to the ancient Roman city of Miletus. Dominating this room (on your right) is the 95-foot-wide, 55-foot-high **Market Gate of Miletus,** destroyed by an earthquake centuries ago and now pains-

BERLIN

takingly reconstructed here in Berlin. The exquisite mosaic floor from a Roman villa in Miletus has two parts: In the square panel, the musician Orpheus strokes his lyre to charm the animals; in stark contrast, in the nearby rectangular mosaic (from an adjacent room), hunters pursue wild animals.

Step through the market gate and all the way back to 575 B.C., to the Fertile Crescent—Mesopotamia (today's Iraq). The Assyrian ruler Nebuchadnezzar II, who amassed a vast empire and enormous wealth, wanted to build a suitably impressive processional entryway to his capital city, Babylon, to honor the goddess Ishtar. His creation, the **Ishtar Gate,** inspired awe and obedience in anyone who came to his city. This is a reconstruction,

using some original components. The gate itself is embellished with two animals: a bull and a mythical dragon-like combination of lion, cobra, eagle, and scorpion. The long hall leading to the main gate—designed for a huge processional of deities to celebrate the new year—is decorated with a chain of blue and yellow glazed tiles with 120 strolling lions (representing the goddess Ishtar). To get the big picture, find the model of the original site in the center of the hall.

These main exhibits are surrounded by smaller galleries. Upstairs is the **Museum of Islamic Art.** It contains fine carpets, tile

work, the Aleppo Room (with ornately painted wooden walls from an early 17th-century home in today's Syria; since it was commissioned by a Christian, it incorporates Arabic, Persian, and biblical themes), and the Mshatta Facade (walls and towers from one of the early eighth-century Umayyad "desert castles," from today's Jordan).

▲▲Neues (New) Museum
Oddly, Museum Island's so-called "new" museum features the oldest stuff around. There are three collections here: the Egyptian Collection (with the famous bust of Queen Nefertiti; floor 0 and

parts of floors 1-2), the Museum of Prehistory and Early History (normally on floor 3, and parts of floors 1-2), and some items from the Collection of Classical Antiquities (artifacts from ancient Troy—famously excavated by German adventurer Heinrich Schliemann—and Cyprus, just off the entrance).

The top draw here is the Egyptian art—clearly one of the world's best collections. But let's face it: The main reason to visit is to enjoy one of the great thrills in art appreciation—gazing into the still young and beautiful face of Queen Nefertiti. If you're in a pinch for time, make a beeline to her (floor 2, far corner of Egyptian Collection in room 210; for more on the museum, see www.neues-museum.de).

Audioguide: The fine audioguide (included with admission) celebrates new knowledge about ancient Egyptian civilization and offers fascinating insights into workaday Egyptian life as it describes the vivid papyrus collection, slice-of-life artifacts, and dreamy wax portraits decorating mummy cases.

Visiting the Museum: After being damaged in World War II and sitting in ruins for some 40 years, the Neues Museum has been rebuilt. Everything is well-described by posted English information and the audioguide.

To tour the whole collection, start at the top (floor 3), which is where you'll find the **prehistory section.** The entire floor is filled with Stone Age, Ice Age, and Bronze Age items. You'll see early human remains, tools, spearheads, and pottery.

The most interesting item on this floor (in corner room 305) is the tall, conehead-like **Golden Hat,** made of paper-thin hammered gold leaf. Created by an early Celtic civilization in Central Europe, it's particularly exquisite for something so old (from the Bronze Age, around 1000 B.C.). The circles on the hat represent the sun, moon, and other celestial bodies—leading archaeologists to believe that this headwear could double as a calendar, showing how the sun and moon sync up every 19 years.

Down on floor 2, you'll find **early history** exhibits on migrations, barbarians, and ancient Rome (including larger-than-life statues of Helios and an unidentified goddess) as well as a fascinating look at the Dark Ages after the fall of Rome.

Still on floor 2, cross to the other side

of the building for the **Egyptian** section. On the way, you'll pass through the impressive Papyrus Collection—a large room of seemingly empty glass cases. Press a button to watch a 3,000-year-old piece of primitive "paper" (made of aquatic reeds) imprinted with primitive text trundle out of its protective home.

Then, finally, in a room all her own, is the 3,000-year-old bust of **Queen Nefertiti** (the wife of King Akhenaton, c. 1340

B.C.)—the most famous piece of Egyptian art in Europe. Called "Berlin's most beautiful woman," Nefertiti has all the right beauty marks: long neck, symmetrical face, and the perfect amount of makeup. And yet, she's not completely idealized. Notice the fine wrinkles that show she's human (though these only enhance her beauty). Like a movie star discreetly sipping a glass of wine at a sidewalk café, Nefertiti seems somehow more dignified in person. The bust never left its studio, but served as a master model for all other portraits of the queen. (That's probably why the left eye was never inlaid.) Stare at her long enough, and you may get the sensation that she's winking at you. Hey, beautiful!

How the queen arrived in Germany is a tale out of *Indiana Jones*. The German archaeologist Ludwig Borchardt uncovered her in the Egyptian desert in 1912. The Egyptian Department of Antiquities had first pick of all the artifacts uncovered on their territory. After the first takings, they divided the rest 50/50 with the excavators. When Borchardt presented Nefertiti to the Egyptians, they passed her over, never bothering to examine her closely. Unsubstantiated rumors persist that Borchardt misled the Egyptians in order to keep the bust for himself—rumors that have prompted some Egyptians to call for the return of Nefertiti (just as the Greeks are lobbying the British to return the Parthenon frieze currently housed in the British Museum). Although this bust is not particularly representative of Egyptian art in general—and despite increasing claims that her long neck suggests she's a Neoclassical fake—Nefertiti has become a symbol of Egyptian art by popular acclaim.

The Egyptian Collection continues with other sculptures, including kneeling figures holding steles (inscribed stone tablets). On floor 1, a fascinating exhibit examines how depictions of the human image evolved during the 3,000-year span of ancient Egyptian culture. You'll also see entire walls from tombs and (in the basement—floor 0) a sea of large sarcophagi.

▲Old National Gallery (Alte Nationalgalerie)

This gallery, behind the Neues Museum and Altes Museum, is designed to look like a Greek temple. Spanning three floors, it

focuses on art (mostly paintings) from the 19th century: Romantic German paintings (which I find most interesting) on the top floor, and French and German Impressionists and German Realists on the first and second floors. You likely won't recognize any specific paintings, but it's still an enjoyable stroll through German culture from the century in which that notion first came to mean something. The included audioguide explains the highlights.

Visiting the Museum: Start on the third floor, with Romantic canvases and art of the Goethe era (roughly 1770-1830), and work

your way down. Use the audioguide to really delve into these romanticized, vivid looks at life in Germany in the 19th century and before. As you stroll through the Romantic paintings—the museum's strength— keep in mind that they were created about the time (mid-late 19th century) that Germans were first working toward a single, unified nation. By glorifying pristine German landscapes and a rugged, virtuous people, these painters evoked the region's high-water mark—the Middle Ages, when "Germany" was a patchwork of powerful and wealthy merchant city-states. Linger over dreamy townscapes with Gothic cathedrals and castles that celebrate medieval German might. Still lifes, idealized portraits of tow-headed children, and genre paintings (depicting everyday scenes, often with subtle social commentary) strum the heartstrings of anyone with Teutonic blood. The Düsseldorf School excelled at Romantic landscapes (such as Carl Friedrich Lessing's *Castle on a Rock*). Some of these canvases nearly resemble present-day fantasy paintings. Perhaps the best-known artist in the collection is Caspar David Friedrich, who specialized in dramatic scenes celebrating grandeur and the solitary hero. His *The Monk by the Sea (Der Mönch am Meer)* shows a lone figure standing on a sand dune, pondering a vast, turbulent expanse of sea and sky.

On the second floor, you'll find one big room of minor works by bigger-name French artists, including Renoir, Cézanne, Manet, Monet, and Rodin. Another room is devoted to the Romantic Hans von Marées, the influential early Symbolist Arnold Böcklin, and other artists of the "German Roman" (Deutschrömer) movement—Germans who lived in, and were greatly influenced by, Rome. Artists of the Munich School are represented by naturalistic canvases of landscapes or slice-of-life scenes.

On the first floor, 19th-century Realism reigns. While the Realist Adolph Menzel made his name painting elegant royal gatherings and historical events, his *Iron Rolling Mill (Das Eisenwalzwerk)* captures the gritty side of his moment in history—the emergence of the Industrial Age—with a warts-and-all look at steelworkers toiling in a hellish factory. The first floor also hosts a sculpture collection, with works by great sculptors both foreign (the Italian Canova, the Dane Thorvaldsen) and German (Johann Gottfried Schadow's delightful *Die Prinzessinnen,* showing the dynamic duo of Prussian princesses, Louise and Frederike). Also on the first floor, near the sculptures, look for a low-key room left unrestored so visitors can recall the days when the DDR ran this museum.

Bode Museum

At the "prow" of Museum Island, the Bode Museum (designed to appear as if it's rising up from the river), is worth a brief stop. Just inside, a grand statue of Frederick William of Brandenburg on horseback, curly locks blowing in the wind, welcomes you into the lonely halls of the museum. This fine building contains a hodgepodge of collections: Byzantine art, historic coins, ecclesiastical art, sculptures, and medals commemorating the fall of the Berlin Wall and German reunification. For a free, quick look at its lavish interior, climb the grand staircase to the charming café on the first floor.

Altes (Old) Museum

Perhaps the least interesting of the five museums, this building features the rest of the Collection of Classical Antiquities—namely, Etruscan, Roman, and Greek art. It also contains Greek and Roman sculptures, vases, and some bronze figurines from the currently closed north wing of the Pergamon Museum.

South of Unter den Linden

The following sights—heavy on Nazi and Wall history—are listed roughly north to south (as you reach them from Unter den Linden).

▲▲Gendarmenmarkt

This delightful, historic square is bounded by twin churches, a tasty chocolate shop, and the Berlin Symphony's concert hall (designed

by Karl Friedrich Schinkel, the man who put the Neoclassical stamp on Berlin and Dresden). In summer, it hosts a few outdoor cafés, *Biergartens,* and sometimes concerts. Wonderfully symmetrical, the square is considered by Berliners to be the finest in town (U6: Französische Strasse; U2 or U6: Stadtmitte).

The name of the square—part French and part German (after the *Gens d'Armes,* Frederick the Great's royal guard, who were headquartered here)—reminds us that in the 17th century, a fifth of all Berliners were French émigrés—Protestant Huguenots fleeing Catholic France. Back then, Frederick the Great's tolerant Prussia was a magnet for the persecuted (and their money). These émigrés vitalized Berlin with new ideas and know-how...and their substantial wealth.

Of the two matching churches on Gendarmenmarkt, the one to the south (bottom end of square) is the **German Cathedral** (Deutscher Dom). This cathedral (not to be confused with the Berlin Cathedral on Museum Island) was bombed flat in the war and rebuilt only in the 1980s. It houses the thought-provoking Milestones, Setbacks, Sidetracks *(Wege, Irrwege, Umwege)* exhibit, which traces the history of the German parliamentary system—worth ▲. The parliament-funded exhibit—while light on actual historical artifacts—is well done and more interesting than it sounds. It takes you quickly from the revolutionary days of 1848 to the 1920s, and then more deeply through the tumultuous 20th century. As the exhibit is designed for Germans rather than foreign tourists, there are no English descriptions—but you can follow the essential, excellent, and free 1.5-hour English audioguide. If you think this museum is an attempt by the German government to develop a more sophisticated and educated electorate in the interest of stronger democracy, you're exactly right. Germany knows (from its own troubled history) that a dumbed-down electorate, manipulated by clever spin-meisters and sound-bite media blitzes, is a dangerous thing (free, Tue-Sun 10:00-19:00, Oct-April until 18:00, closed Mon year-round, tel. 030/2273-0431).

The **French Cathedral** (Französischer Dom), at the north end of the square, offers a humble museum on the Huguenots (€2, Tue-Sun 12:00-17:00, closed Mon, enter around the right side) and a viewpoint in the dome up top (€3, daily March-Dec 10:00-19:00,

Jan-Feb 10:00-18:00, last entry one hour before closing, 244 steps, enter through door facing square, tel. 030/2067-4690, www.franzoesischer-dom.de).

Fun fact: Neither of these churches is a true cathedral, as they never contained a bishop's throne; their German title of *Dom* (cathedral) is actually a mistranslation from the French word *dôme* (cupola).

Fassbender & Rausch, on the corner near the German Cathedral, claims to be Europe's biggest chocolate store. After 150 years of chocolate-making, this family-owned business proudly displays its sweet delights—250 different kinds—on a 55-foot-long buffet. Truffles are sold for about €0.70 each; it's fun to compose a fancy little eight-piece box of your own for about €6. Upstairs is an elegant hot chocolate café with fine views. The

window displays feature giant chocolate models of Berlin landmarks—Reichstag, Brandenburg Gate, Kaiser Wilhelm Memorial Church, and so on. If all this isn't enough to entice you, I have

three words: erupting chocolate volcano (Mon-Sat 10:00-20:00, Sun 11:00-20:00, corner of Mohrenstrasse at Charlottenstrasse 60, tel. 030/2045-8440).

Gendarmenmarkt is buried in what has recently emerged as Berlin's "Fifth Avenue" shopping district. For the ultimate in top-end shops, find the corner of Jägerstrasse and Friedrichstrasse and wander through the **Quartier 206** (Mon-Fri 10:30-19:30, Sat 10:00-18:00, closed Sun, www.quartier206.com). The adjacent, middlebrow **Quartier 205** has more affordable prices.

Nazi and Cold War Sites
A variety of fascinating sites relating to Germany's tumultuous 20th century cluster south of Unter den Linden. While you can see your choice of the following places in any order, I've linked them by way of a short, poignant walk from Potsdamer Platz to Checkpoint Charlie.

• *From Potsdamer Platz, take a few steps down Stresemannstrasse and detour left down Erna-Berger-Strasse to find a lonely concrete watchtower.*

DDR Watchtower

This was one of many such towers built in 1966 for panoramic surveillance and shooting (note the rifle windows, allowing shots to be fired in 360 degrees). It was constantly manned by two guards who were forbidden to get to know each other (no casual chatting)—so they could effectively guard each other from escaping. This is one of only a few such towers still standing.

Cost and Hours: €3.50, daily 14:00-18:00.

• *Return to Stresemannstrasse, and continue south (away from Potsdamer Platz). As you round the corner turning left, you'll begin to see some...*

Fragments of the Wall

Surviving stretches of the Wall are rare in downtown Berlin, but you'll find a few in this area. On the left as you turn from Erna-Berger-Strasse onto Stresemannstrasse, look carefully at the modern Ministry of the Environment (Bundesministerium für Umwelt) building; notice the nicely painted stretch of **inner wall** (inside the modern building constructed around it). The Wall was actually two

walls, with a death strip in the middle (where Stresemannstrasse is today). Across the street, embedded in the sidewalk, you can see cobblestones marking the former path of the outer wall.

At the corner with Niederkirchnerstrasse, turn left and follow the cobbles in the sidewalk. After about a block (just beyond the Martin-Gropius-Bau museum), where the street becomes cobbled, an **original fragment** of the Berlin Wall stretches alongside the right side of the street.

• *Follow the Wall until it ends, at the intersection of Niederkirchnerstrasse and Wilhelmstrasse. Hook right around the end of the Wall to reach the...*

▲▲Topography of Terror (Topographie des Terrors)

Coincidentally, the patch of land behind the surviving stretch of Wall was closely associated with a different regime: It was once the nerve center for the most despicable elements of the Nazi govern-

ment, the Gestapo and the SS. This stark-gray, boxy building is one of the few memorial sites that focuses on the perpetrators rather than the victims of the Nazis. It's chilling but thought-provoking to see just how seamlessly and bureaucratically the Nazi institutions and state structures merged to become a well-oiled terror machine. There are few actual artifacts; it's mostly written explanations and photos, like reading a good textbook standing up. And, while you could read this story anywhere, to take this in atop the Gestapo headquarters is a powerful experience. The exhibit is a bit dense, but WWII historians (even armchair ones) will find it fascinating.

Cost and Hours: Free, includes audioguide for outdoor exhibit, daily 10:00-20:00, outdoor exhibit closes at dusk, Niederkirchnerstrasse 8, tel. 030/254-5090, www.topographie.de.

Background: This location marks what was once the most feared address in Berlin: the headquarters of the Reich Main Security Office *(Reichssicherheitshauptamt)*. These offices served as the engine room of the Nazi dictatorship, as well as the command center of the SS *(Schutzstaffel,* whose members began as Hitler's personal bodyguards), the Gestapo *(Geheime Staatspolizei,* secret state police), and the SD *(Sicherheitsdienst,* the Nazi intelligence agency). This trio (and others) were ultimately consolidated under Heinrich Himmler to become a state-within-a-state, with talons in every corner of German society. This elite militarized branch of the Nazi machine was also tasked with the "racial purification" of German-held lands, especially Eastern Europe—the Holocaust. It was from these headquarters that the Nazis administered concentration camps, firmed up plans for the "Final Solution to the Jewish Question," and organized the domestic surveillance of anyone opposed to the regime. The building was also equipped with dungeons, where the Gestapo detained and tortured thousands of prisoners.

The Gestapo and SS employed intimidation techniques to coerce cooperation from the German people. The general public knew that the Gestapo was to be feared: It was considered omnipotent, omnipresent, and omniscient. Some political prisoners underwent "enhanced interrogation" right here in this building. The threat of *Schutzhaft* ("protective custody," usually at a concentration camp) was used to terrify any civilians who stepped out of line—or who might make a good example. But Hitler and his cronies also won people's loyalties through propaganda. They hammered home the idealistic notion of the *Volksgemeinschaft* ("people's community") of a purely Germanic culture and race, which empowered Hitler to create a pervasive illusion that "We're all in this together." Anyone who was not an Aryan was *Untermensch*—subhuman—and must be treated as such.

Visiting the Museum: The complex has two parts: indoors, in the modern boxy building; and outdoors, in the trench that runs along the surviving stretch of Wall. Visit the indoor exhibit first.

Inside, you'll find a visitors center with an information desk and an extensive **Topography of Terror** exhibit about the SS and

Gestapo, and the atrocities they committed in Berlin and across Europe. A model of the government quarter, circa 1939, sets the stage of Nazi domination in this area. A timeline of events and old photographs, documents, and newspaper clippings illustrates how Hitler and his team expertly manipulated the German people to build a broadly supported "dictatorship of consent."

The exhibit walks you through the evolution of Hitler's regime: the Nazi takeover; institutions of terror (Himmler's "SS State"); ter-

ror, persecution, and extermination; atrocities in Nazi-occupied countries; and the war's end and postwar. Some images here are indelible, such as photos of SS soldiers stationed at Auschwitz, gleefully yukking it up on a retreat in the countryside (even as their helpless prisoners were being gassed and burned a few miles away). The exhibit profiles specific members of the various reprehensible SS branches, as well as the groups they targeted: Jews; Roma and Sinti (Gypsies); the unemployed or homeless; homosexuals; and the physically and mentally ill (considered "useless eaters" who consumed resources without contributing work).

Downstairs is a WC and a library with research books on these topics. Before heading outside, ask at the information desk for the free audioguide that describes the outdoor exhibits.

Outside, in the trench along the Wall, you'll find the exhibit **Berlin 1933-1945: Between Propaganda and Terror** (occasion-

ally replaced by temporary exhibits), which overlaps slightly with the indoor exhibit but focuses on Berlin. The chronological survey begins with the post-WWI Weimar Republic and continues through the ragged days just after World War II.

One display explains how Nazis invented holidays (or injected new Aryan meaning into existing ones) as a means of winning over the public. Other exhibits cover the "Aryanization" of Jewish businesses (they were simply taken over by the state and handed over to new Aryan owners); Hitler's plans for converting Berlin into a gigantic "Welthauptstadt (World Capital) Germania"; and the postwar Berlin Airlift, which brought provisions to some 2.2 million West Berliners whose supply lines were cut off by East Berlin.

With more time, explore the grounds around the blocky building on a **"Site Tour."** Posted signs (and the audioguide) explain 15 different locations, including the scant remains of the prison cellars.

• *Backtrack to Niederkirchnerstrasse. Opposite the Wall remnant is one end of a huge building...*

German Finance Ministry
(Bundesministerium der Finanzen)

The only major Hitler-era government building that survived the war's bombs, this once housed the headquarters of the Nazi Luftwaffe (Air Force). Notice how the whole building gives off a monumental feel, making the average person feel small and powerless. After the war, this was the headquarters for the Soviet occupation. Later the DDR was founded here, and the communists used the building to house their—no joke—Ministry of Ministries.

Walk up Wilhelmstrasse (to the north) to see an entry gate (on your left) that looks much like it did when Germany occupied nearly all of Europe. This courtyard is much used by movie producers needing a Nazi set.

On the north side of the building (farther up Wilhelmstrasse, under the portico at the corner with Leipziger Strasse) is a wonderful example of communist art. The mural, Max Lingner's *Aufbau der Republik* (*Building the Republic,* 1953), is classic Socialist Realism, showing the entire society—industrial laborers, farm workers, women, and children—all happily singing the same patriotic song. Its subtitle: "The importance of peace for the cultural development of humanity and the necessity of struggle to achieve this goal." This was the communist ideal.
For the reality, look at the ground in the courtyard in front of the mural to see an enlarged photograph from a 1953 uprising here against the communists...quite a contrast. Placards explain the events of 1953 in English.

• *Retrace your steps to the Niederkirchnerstrasse intersection and hook left onto Zimmerstrasse to the...*

Stasi Museum

This modest exhibit tells the story of how the communist-era Ministry for State Security (*Staatssicherheit,* a.k.a. Stasi) infiltrated all aspects of German life. Soon after the Wall fell, DDR authorities scrambled to destroy the copious illicit information their agents and informants had collected about the people of East Germany. But the government mandated that these records be preserved as evidence of DDR crimes, and the documents are now managed by the Federal Commissioner for Stasi Records. A timeline traces the history of the archives, and wraparound kiosks profile individual "subversive elements" who were targeted by the Stasi. There are a few actual artifacts, but the exhibit is mostly dryly written texts and reproduced photographs that don't do much to personalize the victims—making this museum worth a visit only for those with a special interest in this period. Temporary exhibits are upstairs.

Cost and Hours: Free, daily 10:00-18:00, Zimmerstrasse 90-91, tel. 030/232-450, www.bstu.bund.de.

Other Stasi Sites: If you're interested in this chapter of East German history, you may find it more satisfying (but time-consuming) to visit two other sites affiliated with the Stasi: a different **Stasi Museum,** in the former State Security headquarters (€5, Mon-Fri 10:00-18:00, Sat-Sun 12:00-18:00, Ruscherstrasse 103, U5: Magdalenenstrasse, tel. 030/553-6854, www.stasimuseum.de); and the **Stasi Prison,** where "enemies of the state" served time (€5, visits possible only with a tour; English tours daily at 14:30—call to confirm before making the trip; German tours hourly Mon-Fri 11:00-15:00, Sat-Sun 10:00-16:00; Genslerstrasse 66, reachable on various trams from downtown—see website for specifics, tel. 030/9860-8230, www.stiftung-hsh.de). There's also a good Stasi Museum in the former State Security branch in Leipzig.

• *On the final stretch of Zimmerstrasse, leading to Checkpoint Charlie, you'll pass several "Ost-algic" business ventures: vendors of DDR soft ice-cream, Trabi World (renting rides in iconic DDR tin-can cars), and the Wall Panorama Exhibition (not worth €10, as it's just huge photos). You'll wind up at...*

▲Checkpoint Charlie

This famous Cold War checkpoint was not named for a person, but for its checkpoint number—as in Alpha (#1, at the East-West

German border, a hundred miles west of here), Bravo (#2, as you enter Berlin proper), and Charlie (#3, the best known because most foreigners passed through here). While the actual checkpoint has long since been dismantled, its former location is home to a fine museum and a mock-up of the original border crossing. The area has become a Cold War freak show and—as if celebrating the final victory of crass capitalism—is one of Berlin's worst tourist-trap zones. A McDonald's stands defiantly overlooking the former haunt of East German border guards. (For a more sober and intellectually redeeming look at the Wall's history, head for the Berlin Wall Memorial at Bernauer Strasse.)

The Berlin Wall (and Its Fall)

The 96-mile-long "Anti-Fascist Protective Rampart," as it was called by the East German government, was erected almost overnight in 1961 to stop the outward flow of people from East to West (3 million had leaked out between 1949 and 1961). The Wall *(Mauer)* was actually two walls; the outer was a 12-foot-high concrete barrier whose rounded, pipe-like top (to discourage grappling hooks) was adorned with plenty of barbed wire. Sandwiched between the walls was a no-man's-land (or "death strip") between 30 and 160 feet wide. More than 100 sentry towers kept a close eye on the Wall. On their way into the death strip, would-be escapees would trip a silent alarm, which alerted sharpshooters.

During the Wall's 28 years, border guards fired 1,693 times and made 3,221 arrests, and there were 5,043 documented successful escapes (565 of these were East German guards). Officially, 136 people were killed at the Wall while trying to escape.

As a tangible, almost too-apt symbol for the Cold War, the Berlin Wall got a lot of attention from politicians both East and West. Two of the 20th century's most repeated presidential quotes were uttered within earshot of the death strip. In 1963, US President John F. Kennedy professed American solidarity with the struggling people of Berlin: *"Ich bin ein Berliner."* A generation later in 1987, with the stiff winds of change already blowing westward from Moscow, President Ronald Reagan issued an ultimatum to his Soviet counterpart: "Mr. Gorbachev, tear down this wall."

The actual fall of the Wall had less to do with presidential proclamations than with the obvious failings of the Soviet system, a general thawing in Moscow (where Gorbachev introduced *perestroika* and *glasnost*, and declared that he would no longer employ force to keep Eastern European satellite states under Soviet rule)—and a bureaucratic snafu.

By November of 1989, it was clear that change was in the air. Hungary had already opened its borders to the West that summer, making it next to impossible for East German authorities to keep people in. A series of anti-regime protests had swept nearby Leipzig a few weeks earlier, attracting hundreds of thousands of supporters. On October 7, 1989—on the 40th anniversary of the official creation of the DDR—East German premier Erich Honecker said, "The Wall will be standing in 50 and even in 100 years." He was only off by 99 years and 11 months. A similar rally in East Berlin's Alexanderplatz on November 4—with a half-million protesters chanting, *"Wir wollen raus!"* (We want out!)—persuaded the East German politburo to begin a gradual process of relaxing travel restrictions.

The DDR's intention was to slightly crack the door to the

West, but an inarticulate spokesman's confusion inadvertently threw it wide open. The decision was made on Thursday, November 9, to tentatively allow a few more Easterners to cross into the West—a largely symbolic reform that was intended to take place gradually, over many weeks. Licking their wounds, politburo members left town early for a long weekend. The announcement about travel restrictions was left to a spokesman, Günter Schabowski, who knew only what was on a piece of paper handed to him moments before he went on television for a routine press conference. At 18:54, Schabowski read the statement dutifully, with little emotion, seemingly oblivious to the massive impact of his own words: "exit via border crossings...possible for every citizen." Reporters, unable to believe what they were hearing, began to prod him about when the borders would open. Schabowski looked with puzzlement at the brief statement, shrugged, and offered his best guess: *"Ab sofort, unverzüglich."* ("Immediately, without delay.")

Schabowski's words spread like wildfire through the streets of both Berlins, its flames fanned by West German TV broadcasts (and Tom Brokaw, who had rushed to Berlin when alerted by NBC's bureau chief). East Berliners began to show up at Wall checkpoints, demanding that border guards let them pass. As the crowds grew, the border guards could not reach anyone who could issue official orders. (The politburo members were effectively hiding out.) Finally, around 23:30, a border guard named Harald Jäger at the Bornholmer Strasse crossing decided to simply open the gates. Easterners flooded into the West, embracing their long-separated cousins, unable to believe their good fortune. Once open, the Wall could never be closed again.

The carnival atmosphere of those first years after the Wall fell is gone, but hawkers still sell "authentic" pieces of the Wall, DDR flags, and military paraphernalia to gawking tourists. When it fell, the Wall was literally carried away by the euphoria. What managed to survive has been nearly devoured by decades of persistent "Wall-peckers."

Americans—the Cold War victors—have the biggest appetite for Wall-related sights, and a few bits and pieces remain for us to seek out. Berlin's best Wall-related sights are the Berlin Wall Memorial along Bernauer Strasse, with a long stretch of surviving Wall (near S-Bahn: Nordbahnhof; page 78), and the Museum of the Wall at Checkpoint Charlie (see page 70). Other stretches of the Wall still standing include the short section at Niederkirchnerstrasse/Wilhelmstrasse (near the Topography of Terror exhibit; page 63) and the longer East Side Gallery (near the Ostbahnhof; page 74).

The rebuilt **guard station** now hosts two actors playing American guards who pose for photos. Notice the larger-than-life **posters** of a young American soldier facing east and a young Soviet soldier facing west. (Look carefully at the "Soviet" soldier. He was photographed in 1999, a decade after there were Soviet soldiers stationed here. He's a Dutch model. His uniform is a nonsensical pile of pins and ribbons with a Russian flag on his shoulder.)

A **photo exhibit** stretches up and down Zimmerstrasse, with great English descriptions telling the story of the Wall. While you could get this information from a book, it's poignant to stand here in person and ponder the gripping history of this place.

A few yards away (on Zimmerstrasse), a **glass panel** describes the former checkpoint. From there, another double row of **cobbles** in Zimmerstrasse shows the former path of the Wall.

Warning: Here and in other places, hustlers charge an exorbitant €10 for a full set of Cold War-era stamps in your passport. Don't be tempted. Technically, this invalidates your passport—which has caused some tourists big problems.

• *Overlooking the chaos of the street scene is the...*

▲▲Museum of the Wall at Checkpoint Charlie (Mauermuseum Haus am Checkpoint Charlie)

While the famous border checkpoint between the American and Soviet sectors is long gone, its memory is preserved by one of Europe's most cluttered museums. During the Cold War, the House at Checkpoint Charlie stood defiantly—spitting distance from the border guards—showing off all the clever escapes over, under, and through the Wall. Today, while the drama is over and hunks of the Wall stand like trophies at its door, the museum survives as a living artifact of the Cold War days. The yellowed descriptions, which have scarcely changed since that time, tinge the museum with nostalgia. It's dusty, disorganized, and overpriced, with lots of reading involved, but all that just adds to this museum's borderline-kitschy charm. If you're pressed for time, this is a decent after-dinner sight.

Cost and Hours: €13, assemble 20 tourists and get in for €8.50 each, €3.50 audioguide, discount with WelcomeCard but not covered by Museumspass, daily 9:30-22:00, U6 to Kochstrasse or—better from Zoo—U2 to Stadtmitte, Friedrichstrasse 43-45, tel. 030/253-7250, www.mauermuseum.de.

Visiting the Museum: Exhibits narrate a gripping history of the Wall, with a focus on the many ingenious **escape attempts** (the early years—with a cruder wall—saw more escapes). You'll see the actual items used to smuggle would-be Wessies: a VW bug whose trunk hid a man, two side-by-side suitcases into which a woman squeezed, a makeshift zip line for crossing over (rather than through) the border, a hot-air balloon in which two families floated to safety (immortalized in the Disney film *Night Crossing*), an inflatable boat that puttered across the dangerous Baltic Sea, primitive homemade aircraft, two surfboards hollowed out to create just enough space for a refugee, and more. One chilling exhibit lists some 43,000 people who died in "Internal Affairs" internment camps during the transition to communism (1945-1950). Profiles personalize various escapees and their helpers, including John P. Ireland, an American who posed as an eccentric antiques collector so he could transport 10 different refugees to safety in his modified Cadillac.

You'll also see **artwork** inspired by the Wall and its fall, and a memorial to Rainer Hildebrandt, who founded this museum shortly after the Wall went up in 1961 (he died in 2004, but the museum lives on as a shrine to his vision). On the **top floor** (easy to miss), that vision broadens to the larger themes of freedom and persecution, including exhibits on Eastern European rebellions (the 1956 uprising in Hungary, 1968's Prague Spring, and the Solidarity movement in 1980s Poland) and Gandhi's protests in India—plus a hodgepodge of displays on world religions and Picasso's *Guernica*. Fans of the "Gipper" appreciate the room honoring President Ronald Reagan, displaying his actual cowboy hat and boots. The small movie theater shows various Wall-related films (a schedule is posted), and the displays include video coverage of those heady days when people power tore down the Wall.

▲▲Jewish Museum Berlin (Jüdisches Museum Berlin)

This museum is one of Europe's best Jewish sights. The highly conceptual building is a sight in itself, and the museum inside—an overview of the rich culture and history of Europe's Jewish community—is excellent, particularly if you take advantage of the informative and engaging audioguide. Rather than just reading dry texts, you'll feel this museum as fresh and alive—an exuberant celebration of the Jewish experience that's accessible to all. Even though the museum is in a nondescript residential neighborhood, it's well worth the trip.

Cost and Hours: €5, €7 for special exhibits, discount with WelcomeCard, daily 10:00-20:00, Mon until 22:00, last entry one hour before closing, closed on Jewish holidays. Tight security includes bag check and metal detectors. The excellent €3 audioguide—with four hours of commentary on 151 different items—is essential to fully appreciate the exhibits. Tel. 030/2599-3300, www.jmberlin.de.

Getting There: Take the U-Bahn to Hallesches Tor, find the exit marked *Jüdisches Museum*, exit straight ahead, then turn right on Franz-Klühs-Strasse. The museum is a five-minute walk ahead on your left, at Lindenstrasse 9.

Eating: The museum's restaurant, Café Schmus, offers good Jewish-style meals, albeit not kosher (daily 10:00-20:00, Mon until 22:00, tel. 030/2579-6751).

Visiting the Museum: Designed by American architect Daniel Libeskind (the master planner for the redeveloped World Trade Center in New York), the zinc-walled building has a zigzag shape pierced by voids symbolic of the irreplaceable cultural loss caused by the Holocaust. Enter the 18th-century Baroque building next door, then go through an underground tunnel to reach the museum interior.

Before you reach the exhibit, your visit starts with three **memorial spaces.** Follow the Axis of Exile to a disorienting slanted garden with 49 pillars (evocative of the Memorial to the Murdered Jews of Europe, across town). Next, the Axis of Holocaust, lined with artifacts from Jews imprisoned and murdered by the Nazis, leads to an eerily empty tower shut off from the outside world. The Axis of Continuity takes you to stairs and the main exhibit. A detour partway up the long stairway leads to the Memory Void, a compelling space of "fallen leaves": heavy metal faces that you walk on, making unhuman noises with each step.

Finish climbing the stairs to the top of the museum, and stroll chronologically through the 2,000-year **story of Judaism** in Germany. The exhibit, on two floors, is engaging, with lots of actual artifacts. Interactive bits (you can, for example, spell your name in Hebrew, or write a prayer and hang it from a tree) make it lively for kids. English explanations interpret both the exhibits and the design of the very symbolic building.

The top floor focuses on everyday life in Ashkenaz (medieval

German-Jewish lands). The nine-minute movie "A Thousand Years Ago" sets the stage for your journey through Jewish history. You'll learn what garlic had to do with early Jews in Germany (hint: It's not just about cooking). The Middle Ages were a positive time for Jewish culture, which flourished then in many areas of Europe. But around 1500, many Jews were expelled from the countryside and moved into cities. Viewing stations let you watch nine short, lively videos that pose provocative questions about faith. Moses Mendelssohn's role in the late-18th-century Jewish Enlightenment, which gave rise to Reform Judaism, is highlighted. The Tradition and Change exhibit analyzes how various subgroups of the Jewish faith modified and relaxed their rules to adapt to a changing world.

Downstairs, on the middle floor, exhibits detail the rising tide of anti-Semitism in Germany through the 19th century—ironically, at a time when many Jews were so secularized that they celebrated Christmas right along with Hanukkah. Berlin's glory days (1890-1933) were a boom time for many Jews, though it was at times challenging to reconcile the reformed ways of the more assimilated western (German) Jews with the more traditional Eastern European Jews. The exhibit segues into the **dark days** of Hitler—the collapse of the relatively tolerant Weimar Republic, the rise of the Nazis, and the horrific night of November 9-10, 1938, when, throughout Germany, hateful mobs destroyed Jewish-owned businesses, homes, synagogues, and even entire villages—called "Crystal Night" (Kristallnacht) for the broken glass that glittered in the streets.

The thought-provoking conclusion brings us to the present day, with the question: How do you keep going after six million of your people have been murdered? You'll see how German society has reacted to the Holocaust blood on its hands (one fascinating exhibit has footage of a 1975 sit-in of German Jews to protest a controversial play with a stereotypical Jewish villain), and listen to headphone commentary of Jewish people describing their experiences growing up in postwar Germany, Austria, and Switzerland.

Karl-Marx-Allee

The buildings along Karl-Marx-Allee in East Berlin (just beyond Alexanderplatz) were completely leveled by the Red Army in 1945. As an expression of their adoration to the "great Socialist Father" (Stalin), the DDR government decided to rebuild the street better than ever (the USSR provided generous subsidies). They intentionally made it one meter wider than the Champs-Elysées, named it Stalinallee, and lined it with "workers' palaces" built in the bold "Stalin Gothic" style so common in Moscow in the 1950s. Now renamed after Karl Marx, the street and its restored buildings provide a rare look at Berlin's communist days. Distances are a bit long for convenient walking, but you can cruise Karl-Marx-Allee by taxi, or ride the U-Bahn to Strausberger Platz (which was built to resemble an Italian promenade) and walk to Frankfurter Tor, reading the good information posts along the way. Notice the Social Realist reliefs on the buildings and the lampposts, which incorporate the wings of a phoenix (rising from the ashes) in their design. Once a "workers' paradise," the street now hosts a two-mile-long capitalist beer festival the first weekend in August.

The **Café Sibylle,** just beyond the Strausberger Platz U-Bahn station, is a fun spot for a coffee, traditional DDR ice-cream treats, and a look at its free informal museum that tells the story of the most destroyed street in Berlin. While the humble exhibit is nearly all in German, it's fun to see the ear (or buy a €10 plaster replica) and half a moustache from what was the largest statue of Stalin in Germany (the centerpiece of the street until 1961). It also provides a few intimate insights into apartment life in a DDR flat. The café is known for its good coffee and *Schwedeneisbecher mit Eierlikor*—an ice-cream sundae with a shot of egg liqueur, popular among those nostalgic for communism (Mon-Fri 10:00-20:00, Sat-Sun 12:00-20:00, Karl-Marx-Allee 72, at intersection with Koppenstrasse, a block from U-Bahn: Strausberger Platz, tel. 030/2935-2203).

Heading out to Karl-Marx-Allee (just beyond the TV Tower), you're likely to notice a giant colorful **mural** decorating a blocky communist-era skyscraper. This was the Ministry of Education, and the mural is a tile mosaic trumpeting the accomplishments of the DDR's version of "No Child Left Behind."

More Sights South of Unter den Linden
East Side Gallery
The biggest remaining stretch of the Wall is now the "world's longest outdoor art gallery." It stretches for nearly a mile and is covered with murals painted by artists from around the world. The murals (classified as protected monuments) got a facelift in 2009, when the city invited the original artists back to re-create their work for the 20th anniversary of the fall of the Wall. This segment of the Wall makes a poignant walk. For a quick look, take the S-Bahn to the Ostbahnhof station (follow signs to Stralauerplatz exit; once outside, TV Tower will be to your right; go left and at next corner look to your right—the Wall is across the busy street). The gallery is slowly being consumed by developers. If you walk the entire length of the East Side Gallery, you'll find a small Wall souvenir shop at the end and a bridge crossing the river to a subway station at Schlesisches Tor (in Kreuzberg). The bridge, a fine example of Brandenburg Neo-Gothic brickwork, has a fun neon "rock, paper, scissors" installment poking fun at the futility of the Cold War (visible only after dark).

Kreuzberg

This district—once abutting the dreary Wall and inhabited mostly by poor Turkish guest laborers and their families—is still run-down, with graffiti-riddled buildings and plenty of student and Turkish street life. It offers a gritty look at melting-pot Berlin, in a city where original Berliners are as rare as old buildings. Berlin is the largest Turkish city outside of Turkey itself, and Kreuzberg is its "downtown." But to call it a "little Istanbul" insults the big one. You'll see *Döner Kebab* stands, shops decorated with spray paint, and mothers wrapped in colorful scarves. But lately, an influx of immigrants from many other countries has diluted the Turkish-ness of Kreuzberg. Berliners come here for fun ethnic eateries. For a colorful stroll, take the U-Bahn to Kottbusser Tor and wander—ideally on Tuesday and Friday between 12:00 and 18:00, when the Turkish Market sprawls along the Maybachufer riverbank. You can sample food specialties or even buy Turkish slippers.

North of Unter den Linden

There are few major sights north of Unter den Linden, but this area has some of Berlin's trendiest, most interesting neighborhoods. I've listed these roughly from south to north, as you'd approach them from the city center and Unter den Linden. On a sunny day, a stroll (or tram ride) through these bursting-with-life areas can be as engaging as any museum in town.

Hackescher Markt

This area, in front of the S-Bahn station of the same name, is a great people scene day and night. The brick trestle supporting the train track is a classic example of the city's Brandenburg Neo-Gothic brickwork. Most of the brick archways are now filled with hip shops, which have official—and newly trendy—addresses such as "S-Bahn Arch #9, Hackescher Markt." Within 100 yards of the S-Bahn station, you'll find recommended Turkish and Bavarian restaurants, walking-tour and pub-crawl departure points, and tram #M1 to Prenzlauer Berg. Also nearby are two fascinating examples of Berlin's traditional courtyards *(Höfe)*—one trendy and modern, the other retro-cool with two fascinating museums.

Hackesche Höfe (a block in front of the Hackescher Markt S-Bahn station, at Rosenthaler Strasse 40) is a series of eight court-yards bunny-hopping through a wonderfully restored 1907 *Jugendstil* (German Art Nouveau) building. Berlin's apartments are organized like this—courtyard after courtyard leading off the main roads. This complex is full of trendy restaurants (including the recommended Turkish eatery, Hasir), theaters, and cinemas (playing movies in their original languages). Courtyard #5 is particularly charming, with a children's park and a DDR shop. This courtyard system is a wonderful example of how to make huge city blocks livable. Two decades after the Cold War, this area has reached the final evolution of East Berlin's urban restoration: total gentrification. These courtyards also offer a useful lesson for visitors: Much of Berlin's charm hides off the street front.

Haus Schwarzenberg, next door (at Rosenthaler Strasse 39), has a totally different feel. This rare surviving bit of East Berlin is owned by an artists' collective, with a bar, cinema (showing art films in their original language), an open-air art space (reminiscent of mid-1990s eastern Berlin), and the basement-level "Dead Chickens" gallery (with far-out hydro-powered art). Its Café Cinema is one of the last remaining '90s bohemian-chic bars. And within this amazing little zone you'll find two inspirational museums. **Museum of Otto Weidt's Workshop for the Blind** (Museum Blindenwerkstatt Otto Weidt) vividly tells the amazing story of a Berliner heroically protecting blind and deaf Jews during World War II (free, daily 10:00-20:00). Otto Weidt employed them to produce brooms and brushes, and because that was useful for the Nazi war machine, he managed to finagle a special status for his workers. You can see the actual brushmaking factory with pedal-powered machines still lined up. The exhibits are well-described (in English and Braille), and there's a good intro video and free audioguide. **Silent Heroes Memorial Center** (Gedenkstätte Stille Helden) is a well-presented exhibit celebrating the quietly courageous individuals who resisted the persecution of the Jews from 1933 to 1945 (free, daily 10:00-18:00).

Oranienburger Strasse

Oranienburger Strasse, a few blocks west of Hackescher Markt, is anchored by an important and somber sight, the New Synagogue (S-Bahn: Oranienburger Strasse). But the rest of this zone (roughly between the synagogue and Torstrasse) is colorful and quirky—especially after dark. The streets behind Grosse Hamburger Strasse flicker with atmospheric cafés, *Kneipen* (pubs), and art galleries. At night (from about 20:00), techno-prostitutes line Oranienburger Strasse. Prostitution is legal throughout Germany. Prostitutes pay taxes and receive health care insurance like anyone else. On this street, they hire security guards (lingering nearby) for safety. The sex workers all seem to buy their Barbarella wardrobes—notice the uniforms complete with matching fanny packs—at the same place.

▲New Synagogue (Neue Synagogue)

A shiny gilded dome marks the New Synagogue, now a museum and cultural center. Consecrated in 1866, this was once the biggest and finest synagogue in Germany, with seating for 3,200 worshippers and a sumptuous Moorish-style interior modeled after the Alhambra. It was desecrated by Nazis on Crystal Night (Kristallnacht) in 1938, bombed in 1943, and partially rebuilt in 1990. Only the dome and facade have been restored—a window overlooks the vacant field marking what used to be the synagogue. On its facade, a small plaque—added by East Berlin Jews in 1966—reads "Never forget" *(Vergesst es nie)*. At that time East Berlin had only a few hundred Jews, but now that the city is reunited, the Jewish community numbers about 12,000.

Inside, past tight security, the small but moving permanent exhibit called Open Ye the Gates describes the Berlin Jewish community through the centuries (filling three big rooms on the ground floor and first floor, with some good English descriptions). Examine the cutaway model showing the entire synagogue (pre-destruction) and an exhibit of religious items. Stairs lead up (past temporary exhibits, with a separate entry fee) to the dome, where there's not much to see except the unimpressive-from-the-inside dome itself and ho-hum views—not worth the entry price or the climb.

Cost and Hours: Main exhibit-€3.50, dome-€2, temporary exhibits-€3, €7 combo-ticket covers everything, audioguide-€3; March-Oct Sun-Mon 10:00-20:00, Tue-Thu 10:00-18:00, Fri 10:00-17:00—until 14:00 in March and Oct; Nov-Feb Sun-Thu 10:00-18:00, Fri 10:00-14:00, closed Sat year-round; Oranienburger Strasse 28/30, enter through the low-profile door in the modern building just right of the domed synagogue facade, S-Bahn: Oranienburger Strasse, tel. 030/8802-8300 and press 1, www.cjudaicum.de.

Eating: Next door to the New Synagogue (to the left as you face it) is every local kid's favorite traditional candy shop, **Bonbonmacherei,** where you can see candy being made the old-fashioned way (Wed-Sat 12:00-20:00, closed Sun-Tue, at Oranienburger Strasse 32, in the Heckmann Höfe—another classic Berlin courtyard). And just around the corner and down the street from the synagogue, you'll find the fully kosher **Beth Café** (closed Sat, Tucholskystrasse 40).

Nearby: A block from the synagogue (to the right as you face it), walk 50 yards down **Grosse Hamburger Strasse** to a little park. This street was known for 200 years as the "street of tolerance" because the Jewish community donated land to Protestants so they could build a church. Hitler turned it into the "street of death" *(Todesstrasse),* bulldozing 12,000 graves of the city's oldest Jewish cemetery and turning a Jewish nursing home into a deportation center. Because of the small but growing radical Islamic element in Berlin, and a smattering of persistent neo-Nazis, several police officers and an Israeli secret agent keep watch over this park and the Jewish high school nearby.

▲The Kennedys Museum

This crisp, private enterprise (in a former Jewish girls' school building that survived the war) delightfully recalls John F. Kennedy's 1963 Germany trip with great photos and video clips as well as a photographic shrine to the Kennedy clan in America. Among the interesting mementos are old campaign buttons and posters, and JFK's notes with the phonetic pronunciation "Ish bin ein Bearleener." Jacqueline Kennedy commented on how strange it was that this—not even in his native language—was her husband's most quotable quote. The highlight: a theater where you can watch a newsreel of Kennedy's historic speech (20 minutes, plays continuously).

Cost and Hours: €5, discount with WelcomeCard, Tue-Sun 11:00-19:00, closed Mon, from Oranienburger Strasse go a block up Tucholskystrasse and turn right to Auguststrasse 13, tel. 030/2065-3570, www.thekennedys.de.

▲▲Berlin Wall Memorial (Gedenkstätte Berliner Mauer)

While tourists flock to Checkpoint Charlie, this memorial is Berlin's most substantial attraction relating to its gone-but-not-forgotten Wall. Exhibits line up

along four blocks of Bernauer Strasse, stretching northeast from the Nordbahnhof S-Bahn station. You can enter two different museums plus various open-air exhibits and memorials, see several fragments of the Wall, and peer from an observation tower down into a preserved, complete stretch of the Wall system (as it was during the Cold War).

Over the next few years, the Memorial plans to gradually add more open-air exhibitions farther along Bernauer Strasse. Eventually the chain of sights will stretch all the way to Eberswalder Strasse and Oderberger Strasse, near the heart of Prenzlauer Berg.

Cost and Hours: Free; Visitor Center and Documentation Center open April-Oct Tue-Sun 9:30-19:00, Nov-March until 18:00, closed Mon year-round; outdoor areas accessible 24 hours daily; last English movie starts at 18:00, memorial chapel closes at 17:00; Bernauer Strasse 111, tel. 030/4679-86666, www.berliner-mauer-gedenkstaette.de.

Stolpersteine (Stumbling Stones)

As you wander through the Hackesche Höfe and Oranienburger Strasse neighborhoods—and throughout Germany—you might stumble over small brass plaques in the sidewalk called *Stolpersteine*. *Stolpern* means "to stumble," which is what you are meant to do. These plaques are placed in front of the homes of residents who were killed during World War II. The *Stolpersteine* serve not only to honor the victims, but also to stimulate thought and discussion on a daily basis (rather than only during visits to memorial sites) and to put an individual's name on the mass horror.

More than 25,000 of these plaques have been installed across Germany. They're made of brass so they stay polished as you walk over them, instead of fading into the sidewalk. On each plaque is the name of the victim who lived in that spot, and how and where that person died. While some Holocaust memorials formerly used neutral terminology like "perished," now they use words like "murdered"—part of the very honest way in which today's Germans are dealing with their country's past. The city of Munich, however, has banned *Stolpersteine*, saying that the plaques were insulting and degrading to victims of persecution, who would continue to be trod on by "Nazi boots." Installation of a *Stolperstein* can be sponsored for €95 and has become popular in schools, where students research the memorialized person's life as a class project.

Getting There: Take the S-Bahn (line S-1, S-2, or S-25—all handy from Potsdamer Platz, Brandenburger Tor, or Friedrichstrasse) to the Nordbahnhof. The Nordbahnhof's underground hallways have history exhibits in English (explained later). Exit by following signs for *Bernauer Strasse,* and you'll pop out across the street from a long chunk of Wall and kitty-corner from the Visitor Center.

Background: The Berlin Wall, which was erected virtually overnight in 1961, ran right along Bernauer Strasse. People were suddenly separated from their neighbors across the street. This stretch was particularly notorious because existing apartment buildings were incorporated into the structure of the Wall itself. Film

footage and photographs from the era show Berliners worriedly watching workmen seal off these buildings from the West, brick by brick. Some people attempted to leap to freedom from upper-story windows, with mixed results. One of the unfortunate ones was Ida Siekmann, who fell to her death from her third-floor apartment on August 22, 1961, and is considered the first casualty of the Berlin Wall.

Visiting the Memorial: From the Nordbahnhof station (which has some interesting Wall history in itself), head first to the Visitor Center to get your bearings, then explore the assorted Wall fragments and other sights in the park across the street. Work your way up Bernauer Strasse to the Documentation Center, Wall System, and memorial chapel.

Nordbahnhof

This S-Bahn station was one of the "ghost stations" of Cold War Berlin. It was built in 1926, closed in 1961, and opened again in 1989. As it was a dogleg of the East mostly surrounded by the West, Western subway trains had permission to use the underground tracks to zip through this station (without stopping, of course) en route between stops in the West. Posted information boards show photos comparing 1989 with 2009, and explain that East German border guards, who were stationed here to ensure that nobody got on or off those trains, were literally locked into their surveillance rooms to prevent them from escaping. (But one subway employee and his family used the tunnels to walk to the West and freedom.)

Follow signs down a long yellow hall to Bernauer Strasse. Climbing the stairs up to the Bernauer Strasse exit, ponder that the doorway at the top of these stairs (marked by the *Sperrmauer 1961-1989* plaque) was a bricked-off no-man's-land just 25 years ago. Stepping outside, you'll see the Wall park (directly across the street) and the Visitor Center (in a low rust-colored building kitty-corner across the street).

Visitor Center (Bezucherzentrum)

This small complex has a helpful information desk, a bookstore, and two good movies that provide context for a visit (they run in English at the top of each hour, about 30 minutes for the whole spiel): *History of the Wall* offers a great 12-minute overview of why the Wall was built and how it fell. That's followed by *Walled In!*, an animated 12-minute film illustrating the Wall as it functioned here at Bernauer Strasse (Wall wonks will find it fascinating). Before leaving, pick up the brochure explaining the outdoor exhibits.

Wall Fragments and Other Sights

Across the street from the Visitor Center is a long stretch of Wall. The park behind it is scattered with a few more Wall chunks as well as monuments and memorials honoring its victims. To get your bearings, find the small model of the entire area when the Wall still stood (just across the street from the Nordbahnhof). While most items are explained by English plaques, the brochure from the Visitor Center helps you better appreciate what you're seeing. The rusty

"Window of Remembrance" monument honors slain would-be escapees with their names, dates of death, and transparent photos viewable from both sides. Before it was the no-man's-land between the walls, this area was the parish graveyard for a nearby church; ironically, DDR officials had to move a thousand graves from here to create a "death strip."

Berlin Wall Documentation Center (Dokumentationszentrum Berliner Mauer)

This "Doku-Center" has two movies, a small exhibit, and a viewpoint tower overlooking the preserved Wall section. The two **films** shown on the ground floor are different from those screened at the Visitor Center: *The View*, dating from 1965, tells the story of an elderly West Berlin woman who lived near the Wall, and could look into the death strip and the East from her window (in German only). *Mauerflug* features aerial photography of Berlin from the spring of 1990—after the Wall had opened, but while most of the 96-mile-long barricade still stood, offering an illuminating look at a divided city (English subtitles).

Upstairs is an **exhibit** with photos and videos detailing the construction of the Wall, which began August 13, 1961. At the model of the Wall along Bernauer Strasse, notice how existing buildings were incorporated into the structure. Headphones let you listen to propagandistic, high-spirited oompah music from East Germany that celebrated the construction of the Wall: "It was high time!" There's also a list of the 163 people who died attempting to cross the Wall. From the top-floor **viewpoint** look down at the Wall itself (described next).

Wall System

This is the last surviving intact bit of the complete "Wall system" (with both sides of its Wall—capped by the round pipe that made it tougher for escapees to get a grip—and its no-man's-land, or death strip). The guard tower came from a different part of the Wall; it was actually purchased on that great capitalist invention, eBay (somewhere, Stalin spins in his grave). A strip of photos and descriptions explains what you're seeing. Plaques along the sidewalk below you mark the locations of escapes or deaths.

Just beyond the Wall section (to the left), and also viewable from the tower, is a modern, cagelike church (described next).

Chapel of Reconciliation (Kapelle der Versöhnung)

This chapel marks the spot of the late-19th-century Church of Reconciliation, which survived WWII bombs—but did not survive the communists. Notice the larger footprint of the original church in the field around the chapel. When the Wall was built, the church wound up, unusable, right in the middle of the death strip. It was torn down in 1985, supposedly because it got in the way of the border guards' sight

lines. (This coincided with a period in which anti-DDR opposition movements were percolating in Christian churches, prompting the atheistic regime to destroy several houses of worship.) If you're interested, walk around the chapel for a closer look (closes at 17:00). The carved wooden altarpiece was saved from the original structure. The chapel hosts daily prayer services for the victims of the Wall.

▲Prenzlauer Berg

Young, in-the-know locals agree that Prenzlauer Berg is one of Berlin's most colorful neighborhoods. The heart of this area, with the trendiest array of cafés, restaurants, boutiques, and street life, is roughly between Helmholtzplatz and Kollwitzplatz and along Kastanienallee (U2: Senefelderplatz and Eberswalder Strasse; or take the S-Bahn to Hackescher Markt and catch tram #M1 north). Similar outposts to the south—closer to Museum Island and Unter den Linden—cluster near the Hackescher Markt S-Bahn station; Rosenthaler Platz U-Bahn station; and Oranienburger Strasse (near the New Synagogue).

"Der Berg," as Berliners call it, was largely untouched during World War II, but its buildings slowly rotted away under the communists. Then, after the Wall fell, it was overrun first with artists and anarchists, then with laid-back hipsters, energetic young families, and clever entrepreneurs who breathed life back into its classic old apartment blocks, deserted factories, and long-forgotten breweries.

Years of rent control kept things affordable for its bohemian residents. But now landlords are free to charge what the market will bear, and the vibe is changing. This is ground zero for Berlin's baby boom: Tattooed and pierced young moms and dads, who've joined the modern rat race without giving up their alternative flair, push their youngsters in designer strollers past trendy boutiques and restaurants.

There are no real sights—just a lively, laid-back neighborhood ignoring its wonderful late-19th-century architecture high overhead. The intersection of Oderberger Strasse and Kastanienallee is a typically convivial bit of Prenzlauer Berg to explore.

If you walk west to the end of Oderberger Strasse, you'll hit the **Wall Park** (Mauerpark). Once part of the Wall's death strip, today it's a Prenzlauer Berg green space—an alternative promenade. The park is particularly entertaining on Sundays, when it hosts a flea market and a giant karaoke party. Along the bluff runs a bit of the Wall covered in graffiti art. Just beyond that is the Friedrich-Ludwig-Jahn-Sportpark stadium from DDR times, built to host the World Youth Festival in 1951 and still marked by its original bombastic light towers (even light towers were designed to stir young communist souls).

Berliners have a strong sense of community. They manage in a big city by enjoying a strong neighborhood identity in areas like Prenzlauer Berg. But there is some tension these days, as locals complain about the cafés and bars catering to yuppies sipping prosecco, while the working class and artistic types are being priced out.

While it has changed plenty, I find Prenzlauer Berg a celebration of life and a joy to stroll through. It's a fun area to explore and have a meal or spend the night.

More Sights North of Unter den Linden

Palace of Tears (Tränenpalast) at Friedrichstrasse Station

The border station attached to Berlin's Friedrichstrasse train station was where Westerners visiting loved ones in the East would be checked before crossing back into the free world. The scene of so many sad farewells, it earned the nickname Tränenpalast, or "palace of tears." It was finally closed in 1990, but the 1962 building survives. An exhibit shows everyday life in a divided Germany, giving a fascinating peek into the paranoid border-control world of the DDR.

Cost and Hours: Free, includes audioguide, Tue-Fri 9:00-19:00, Sat-Sun 10:00-18:00, closed Mon, on the river side of the Friedrichstrasse station, Reichstagufer 17, www.hdg.de/berlin.

Natural History Museum (Museum für Naturkunde)

This museum is worth a visit just to see the largest dinosaur skeleton ever assembled. While you're there, meet "Bobby" the stuffed ape, and tour the Wet Collections, displaying shelf after shelf of animals preserved in ethanol (about a million all together). The museum is a magnet for the city's children, who love the interactive displays, the "History of the Universe in 120 Seconds" exhibit, and the cool virtual-reality "Jurascope" glasses that put meat and skin on all the dinosaur skeletons.

Cost and Hours: €6, €3.50 for kids, discount with WelcomeCard, Tue-Fri 9:30-18:00, Sat-Sun 10:00-18:00, closed Mon, Invalidenstrasse 43, U6: Naturkundemuseum, tel. 030/2093-8591, www.naturkundemuseum-berlin.de.

Sights in Central Berlin

Tiergarten Park and Nearby

Berlin's "Central Park" stretches two miles from Bahnhof Zoo to the Brandenburg Gate.

Victory Column (Siegessäule)

The Tiergarten's newly restored centerpiece, the Victory Column, was built to commemorate the Prussian defeat of Denmark in 1864...then reinterpreted after the defeat of France in 1870. The pointy-helmeted Germans rubbed it in, decorating the tower with French cannons and paying for it all with francs received as war reparations. The three lower rings commemorate Bismarck's victories. I imagine the statues of Moltke and other German military greats—which lurk among the trees nearby—goose-stepping around the floodlit angel at night.

Originally standing at the Reichstag, in 1938 the tower was moved to this position and given a 25-foot lengthening by Hitler's architect, Albert Speer, in anticipation of the planned re-envisioning of Berlin as "Welthauptstadt Germania"—the capital of a worldwide Nazi empire. Streets leading to the circle are flanked by surviving Nazi guardhouses, built in the stern style that fascists loved. At the memorial's first level, notice how WWII bullets chipped the fine marble columns. From 1989 to 2003, the column was the epicenter of the Love Parade (Berlin's city-wide techno-hedonist street party), and it was the backdrop for Barack Obama's summer 2008 visit to Germany as a presidential candidate.

Climbing its 270 steps earns you a breathtaking Berlin-wide view and a close-up of the gilded bronze statue of the goddess Victoria. You might recognize Victoria from Wim Wenders' 1987 art-house classic *Wings of Desire*, or the *Stay (Faraway, So Close!)* video he directed for the rock band U2.

Cost and Hours: €3, daily April-Oct 9:30-18:30, Nov-March 10:00-17:00, closes in the rain, no elevator, bus #100, tel. 030/8639-8560.

Flea Market

A colorful flea market thrives weekends on Strasse des 17 Juni, with great antiques, more than 200 stalls, collector-savvy merchants, and fun German fast-food stands (Sat-Sun 6:00-16:00, right next to S-Bahn: Tiergarten).

German Resistance Memorial
(Gedenkstätte Deutscher Widerstand)

This memorial and museum, located in the former Bendlerblock military headquarters just south of the Tiergarten, tells the story of several organized German resistance movements and the more than 42 separate assassination attempts against Hitler. An ill-fated scheme to kill Hitler was plotted in this building (the actual attempt occurred in Rastenburg, eastern Prussia; the event was dramatized in the 2009 Tom Cruise film *Valkyrie*). The conspirators, including Claus Schenk Graf von Stauffenberg, were shot here in the courtyard. While there are no real artifacts, the spirit that haunts the place is multilingual.

Cost and Hours: Free, Mon-Fri 9:00-18:00, Thu until 20:00, Sat-Sun 10:00-18:00, free and good English audioguide—passport required, €3 printed English translation, no crowds, near Kulturforum at Stauffenbergstrasse 13, enter in courtyard, door on left, main exhibit on third floor, bus #M29, tel. 030/2699-5000, www.gdw-berlin.de.

Potsdamer Platz and Nearby

The "Times Square of Berlin," and possibly the busiest square in Europe before World War II, Potsdamer Platz was cut in two by the Wall and left a deserted no-man's-land for 40 years. Today, this immense commercial/residential/entertainment center, sitting on a futuristic transportation hub, is home to the European corporate headquarters of several big-league companies.

▲Potsdamer Platz

The new Potsdamer Platz was a vision begun in 1991, the year that Germany's parliament voted to relocate the seat of government to Berlin. Since then, Sony, Daimler, and other major corporations have turned the square once again into a city center. Like great Christian churches built upon pagan holy grounds, Potsdamer Platz—with its corporate logos flying high and shiny above what was the Wall—trumpets the triumph of capitalism.

While Potsdamer Platz tries to give Berlin a common center, the city has always been—and remains—a collection of towns. Locals recognize 28 distinct neighborhoods that may have grown together but still maintain their historic orientation. While Munich has the single dominant Marienplatz, Berlin will always have Charlottenburg, Savignyplatz, Kreuzberg, Prenzlauer Berg, and so on. In general, Berliners prefer these characteristic neighborhoods to an official city center. They're unimpressed by the grandeur of Potsdamer Platz, simply considering it a good place to go to the movies, with overpriced, touristy restaurants.

While most of the complex just feels big (the arcade is like any huge, modern, American mall), the entrance to the complex and Sony Center are worth a visit, and German-film buffs will enjoy the Deutsche Kinemathek museum (described later).

For an overview of the new construction, and a scenic route to the Sony Center, start at the Bahnhof Potsdamer Platz (east end of Potsdamer Strasse, S-Bahn and U-Bahn: Potsdamer Platz, exit following *Leipziger Platz* signs to see the best view of skyscrapers as you emerge). Find the green hexagonal **clock tower** with the traffic lights on top. This is a replica of the first electronic traffic light in Europe, which once stood at the six-street intersection of Potsdamer Platz. (The traffic cops who stood with flag and trumpet in the middle of the intersection were getting hit by cars too routinely, so this perch was built for them.)

On either side of Potsdamer Strasse, you'll see enormous cubical entrances to the underground Potsdamer Platz train station. Near these entrances, notice the slanted **glass cylinders** sticking out of the ground. The mirrors on the tops of the tubes move with the sun to collect light and send it underground (saving piles of euros in energy costs). A line in the pavement indicates where the **Berlin Wall** once stood (it traces about 25 miles of the wall through the city). On the right side of the street, notice the re-erected slabs of the Wall. Imagine when the first piece was cut out (see photo and history on nearby panel). These hang like scalps at the gate of Fort Capitalism...look up at the towering corporate headquarters: Market forces have won a clear victory. Now descend into one of the train station entrances and follow signs to *Sony Center*. As you walk through the passage, notice the wall panels with historical information.

You'll come up the escalator into the **Sony Center** under a grand canopy (designed to evoke Mount Fuji). At night, multicolored floodlights play on the underside of this tent. Office workers

and tourists eat here by the fountain, enjoying the parade of people. The modern Bavarian Lindenbräu beer hall—the Sony boss wanted a *Bräuhaus*—serves traditional food (€11-19, daily 11:00-24:00, big €11 salads, three-foot-long taster boards of eight different beers, tel. 030/2575-1280). Across the plaza, Josty Bar is built around a surviving bit of a venerable hotel that was a meeting place for Berlin's rich and famous before the bombs (€12-20 meals, daily 8:00-24:00, tel. 030/2575-1105). CineStar is a rare cinema that plays mainstream movies in their original language (www.cinestar.de).

A huge **screen** above the Deutsche Kinemathek museum (left of Starbucks) shows big sporting events on special occasions. Otherwise it runs historic video clips of Potsdamer Platz through the decades.

Sights near Potsdamer Platz
▲Deutsche Kinemathek Film and TV Museum
This exhibit is the most interesting place to visit in the Sony Center. The early pioneers in filmmaking were German (including Fritz Lang, F. W. Murnau, Ernst Lubitsch, and the Austrian-born Billy Wilder), and many of them also became influential in Hollywood—making this a fun visit for cinephiles. Your admission ticket gets you into several floors of exhibits (including temporary exhibits on floors 1 and 4) made meaningful by the included, essential English audioguide.

Cost and Hours: €7, free Thu 16:00-20:00, includes 1.5-hour audioguide, Tue-Sun 10:00-18:00, Thu until 20:00, closed Mon, tel. 030/2474-9888, www.deutsche-kinemathek.de.

Nearby: The Kino Arsenal theater downstairs shows offbeat art-house films in their original language.

Visiting the Museum: From the ticket desk, ride the elevator up to the third floor, where you can turn left (into the film section, floors 3 and 2) or right (into the TV section, floors 3 and 4).

In the **film section,** you'll walk back in time through a fun mirrored entryway. The exhibit starts with the German film industry's beginnings, with an emphasis on the Weimar Republic period in the 1920s, when Berlin rivaled Hollywood. Influential films included the early German Expressionist masterpiece *The Cabinet of Dr. Caligari* (1920) and Fritz Lang's seminal *Metropolis* (1927). Three rooms are dedicated to Marlene Dietrich, who was a huge star both in Germany and, later, in Hollywood. (Dietrich, who performed at USO shows to entertain Allied troops fighting against her former homeland, once said, "I don't hate the Germans, I hate the Nazis.") Another section examines Nazi use of film as propaganda, including Leni Riefenstahl's masterful documentary of the 1936 Berlin Olympics and her earlier, chillingly propagandistic *Triumph des Willens (Triumph of the Will,* 1935). The postwar period was defined by two separate East and West German film industries. The exhibit's finale reminds us that German filmmakers are still highly influential and successful—including Wolfgang Petersen *(Das Boot, Air Force One, The Perfect Storm)* and Werner Herzog (documentaries such as *Grizzly Man,* and the drama *Rescue Dawn*). If this visit gets you curious about German cinema, see the recommendations in the Appendix.

The **TV section** tells the story of *das Idioten Box* from its infancy (when it was primarily used as a Nazi propaganda tool) to today. The 30-minute kaleidoscopic review—kind of a frantic fast-forward montage of greatest hits in German TV history, both East and West—is great fun even if you don't understand a word of it (it plays all day long, with 10-minute breaks). Otherwise, the TV section is a little more challenging for non-German speakers to appreciate. Upstairs (on the fourth floor) is a TV archive where you can dial through a wide range of new and classic German TV standards.

Panoramapunkt

Across Potsdamer Strasse from the Film and TV Museum, you can ride what's billed as the "fastest elevator in Europe" to skyscraping rooftop views. You'll travel at nearly 30 feet per second to the top of the 300-foot-tall Kollhoff Tower. Its sheltered but open-air view deck provides a fun opportunity to survey Berlin's ongoing construction from above.

Cost and Hours: €5.50, €9.50 VIP ticket lets you skip the line, audioguide-€2.50, daily 10:00-20:00, until 22:00 in summer, last elevator 30 minutes before closing, in red-brick building at Potsdamer Platz 1, tel. 030/2593-7080, www.panorama punkt.de.

Kulturforum

Just west of Potsdamer Platz, Kulturforum rivals Museum Island as the city's cultural heart, with several top museums and Berlin's concert hall—home of the world-famous Berlin Philharmonic orchestra. Of its sprawling museums, only the Gemäldegalerie is a must.

Combo-Tickets: All Kulturforum sights are covered by a single €12 Bereichskarte Kulturforum combo-ticket—a.k.a. Quartier-Karte—and by the Museumspass, www.kulturforum-berlin.de.

Getting There: Ride the S-Bahn or U-Bahn to Potsdamer Platz, then walk along Potsdamer Platz; or from Bahnhof Zoo, take bus #200 to Philharmonie.

▲▲Gemäldegalerie

Literally the "Painting Gallery," Germany's top collection of 13th-through 18th-century European paintings (more than 1,400 canvases) is beautifully displayed in a building that's a work of art in itself. The North Wing starts with German paintings of the 13th to 16th century, including eight by Albrecht Dürer. Then come the Dutch and Flemish—Jan van Eyck, Pieter Brueghel, Peter Paul Rubens, Anthony van Dyck, Frans Hals, and Jan Vermeer. The wing finishes with German, English, and French 18th-century artists, such as Thomas Gainsborough and Antoine Watteau. An octagonal hall at the end features an impressive stash of Rembrandts. The South Wing is saved for the Italians—Giotto, Botticelli, Titian, Raphael, and Caravaggio.

Cost and Hours: €10, covered by Kulturforum combo-ticket and Museumspass, Tue-Sun 10:00-18:00, Thu until 20:00, closed Mon, audioguide included with entry, clever little loaner stools, great salad bar in cafeteria upstairs, Matthäikirchplatz 4, tel. 030/266-424-242, www.smb.museum.

❍ Self-Guided Tour: I'll point out a few highlights, focusing on Northern European artists (German, Dutch, and Flemish), with a few Spaniards and Italians thrown in. To go beyond my selections, make ample use of the excellent audioguide.

The collection spreads out on one vast floor surrounding a central hall. Inner rooms have Roman numerals (I, II, III), while adjacent outer rooms are numbered (1, 2, 3). After showing your ticket, turn right into room I and work your way counterclockwise (and roughly chronologically) through the collection.

Rooms I-III/1-4 kick things off with early German paintings (13th-16th century). In Room 1, look for the 1532 portrait of wealthy Hanseatic cloth merchant Georg Gisze by **Hans Hol-**

bein the Younger (1497-1543). Gisze's name appears on several of the notes stuck to the wall behind him. And, typical of detail-rich Northern European art, the canvas is bursting with highly symbolic tidbits. Items scattered on the tabletop and on the shelves behind the merchant represent his lofty status and aspects of his life story. In the vase, the carnation represents his recent engagement, and the herbs symbolize his virtue. And yet, the celebratory flowers have already begun to fade and the scales behind him are unbalanced, reminders of the fleetingness of happiness and wealth.

In Room 2 are fine portraits by the remarkably talented **Albrecht Dürer** (1471-1528), who traveled to Italy during the burgeoning days of the early Renaissance and melded the artistic harmony and classical grandeur he discovered there with a Northern European attention to detail. In his *Portrait of Hieronymus Holzschuher* (1526), Dürer skillfully captured the personality of a friend from Nürnberg, right down to the sly twinkle in his sidelong glance. Technically the portrait is perfection: Look closely and see each individual hair of the man's beard and fur coat, and even the reflection of the studio's windows in his eyes. Also notice Dürer's little pyramid-shaped, D-inside-A signature. Signing one's work was a revolutionary assertion of Dürer's renown at a time when German artists were considered anonymous craftsmen.

Lucas Cranach the Elder (1472-1553), whose works are in Room III, was a court painter for the prince electors of Saxony

and a close friend of Martin Luther (and his unofficial portraitist). But *The Fountain of Youth* (1546) is a far cry from Cranach's solemn portrayals of the Reformer. Old women helped to the fountain (on the left) emerge as young ladies on the right. Newly nubile, the women go into a tent to dress up, snog with noblemen in the bushes (right foreground), dance merrily beneath the trees, and dine grandly beneath a landscape of phallic mountains and towers. This work is flanked by Cranach's Venus nudes. I sense a pattern here.

Netherlandish painters (Rooms IV-VI/4-7) were early adopt-

ers of oil paint (as opposed to older egg tempera), whose relative ease of handling allowed them to brush the super-fine details for which they are famous. **Rogier van der Weyden** (Room IV) was a virtuoso of the new medium. In *Portrait of a Young Woman* (c. 1400-1464), the subject wears a typical winged bonnet, addressing the viewer directly with her fetching blue eyes. The subjects (especially women) of most portraits of the time look off to one side; some art historians guess that the confident woman shown here is Van der Weyden's wife. In the same room is a remarkable, rare trio of three-panel altarpieces by Van der Weyden: The *Marienaltar* shows the life of the Virgin Mary; the *Johannesaltar* narrates the life of John the Baptist—his birth, baptizing Christ (with God and the Holy Spirit hovering overhead), and his gruesome death by decapitation; and the *Middelburger Altar* tells the story of the Nativity. Savor the fine details in each panel of these altarpieces.

Flash forward a few hundred years to the 17th century and Flemish (Belgian) painting (Rooms VII-VIII/9-10), and it's appar-

ent how much the Protestant Reformation—and resulting Counter-Reformation—changed the tenor of Northern European art. In works by **Peter Paul Rubens** (1577-1640)—including *Jesus Giving Peter the Keys to Heaven*—calm, carefully studied, detail-oriented seriousness gives way to an exuberant Baroque trumpeting of the greatness of the Catholic Church. In the Counter-Reformation world, the Catholic Church had serious competition for the hearts and minds of its congregants. Exciting art like this became a way to keep people in the pews. Notice the quivering brushstrokes and almost too-bright colors. (In the same room are portraits by Rubens' student, Anthony van Dyck, as well as some hunting still lifes from Frans Snyders and others.) In the next rooms (VIII and 9) are more Rubens, including the mythological *Perseus Freeing Andromeda* and *The Martyrdom of St. Sebastian by Arrows* (loosely based on a more famous rendition by Andrea Mantegna).

Dutch painting from the 17th century (Rooms IX-XI/10-19) is dominated by the convivial portraits by **Frans Hals** (c. 1582-

1666). His 1620 portrait of Catharina Hooft (far corner, Room 13) presents a startlingly self-possessed baby (the newest member of a wealthy merchant family) dressed with all the finery of a queen, adorned with lace and jewels, and clutching a golden rattle. The smiling

nurse supporting the tyke offers her a piece of fruit, whose blush of red perfectly matches the nanny's apple-fresh cheeks.

But the ultimate Dutch master is **Rembrandt van Rijn** (1606-1669), whose powers of perception and invention propelled him to fame in his lifetime. Displayed here are several storytelling scenes (Room 16), mostly from classical mythology or biblical stories, all employing Rembrandt's trademark chiaroscuro technique (with a strong contrast between light and dark). In *The Rape of Persephone*, Pluto grabs Persephone from his chariot and races toward the underworld, while other goddesses cling to her robe, trying to save her. Cast against a nearly black background, the almost overexposed, action-packed scene is shockingly emotional. In the nearby *Samson and Delilah* (1628), Delilah cradles Samson's head in her lap while silently signaling to a goon to shear Samson's hair, the secret to his strength. A self-portrait (Room X) of a 28-year-old Rembrandt wearing a beret is paired with the come-hither 1637 *Portrait of Hendrickje Stoffels* (the two were romantically linked). *Samson Threatens His Father-in-Law* (1635) captures the moment just after the mighty Samson (with his flowing hair, elegant robes, and shaking fist) has been told by his wife's father to take a hike. I wouldn't want to cross this guy.

Although **Johannes Vermeer** (1632-1675) is today just as admired as Rembrandt, he was little known in his day, probably

because he painted relatively few works for a small circle of Delft collectors. Vermeer was a master at conveying a complicated story through a deceptively simple scene with a few poignant details—whether it's a woman reading a letter at a window, a milkmaid pouring milk from a pitcher into a bowl, or (as in *The Glass of Wine*, Room 18) a young man offering a drink to a young lady. The young man had been playing her some music on his lute (which now sits, discarded, on a chair) and is hoping to seal the deal with some alcohol. The woman is finishing one glass of wine, and her would-be suitor stands ready—almost *too* ready—to pour her another. His sly, somewhat smarmy smirk drives home his high hopes for what will come next. Vermeer has perfectly captured the exact moment of "Will she or won't she?" The painter offers some clues—the coat of arms in the window depicts a woman holding onto the reigns of a horse, staying in control—but ultimately, only he (and the couple) know how this scene will end.

Shift south to Italian, French, and Spanish painting of the 17th and 18th centuries (Rooms XII-XIV/23-28). Venetian cityscapes by Canaletto (who also painted Dresden) and lots of bombastic Baroque art hang in Room

XII. Room XIII features big-name Spanish artists Murillo, Zurbarán, and the great **Diego Velázquez** (1599-1660). He gave the best of his talents to his portraits, capturing warts-and-all likenesses that are effortlessly real. His 1630 *Portrait of a Lady* conveys the subject's subtle, sly Mona Lisa smile. Her figure and face (against a dull gray background) are filtered through a pleasant natural light. Notice that if you stand too close, the brushstrokes get muddy—but when you back up, the scene snaps into perfectly sharp relief.

From here, the collection itself takes a step backwards—into Italian paintings of the 13th-16th century (Rooms XV-XVIII/29-41). This section includes some lesser-known works by great Italian Renaissance painters, including Raphael (Rooms XVII and 29, including five different Madonnas, among them the *Terranuova Madonna*, in a round frame) and Sandro Botticelli (Room VIII).

New National Gallery (Neue Nationalgalerie)

This gallery features 20th-century art, with ever-changing special exhibits. The building, which opened in 1968, was the last commission completed by esteemed architect Ludwig Mies van der Rohe.

Cost and Hours: Covered by Kulturforum combo-ticket and Museumspass, Tue-Fri 10:00-18:00, Thu until 20:00, Sat-Sun 11:00-18:00, closed Mon, café downstairs, Potsdamer Strasse 50, tel. 030/266-424-242, www.smb.museum.

Museum of Decorative Arts (Kunstgewerbemuseum)

This newly renovated museum is scheduled to reopen in the spring of 2014. Wander through a thousand years of applied arts—porcelain, fine *Jugendstil* (German Art Nouveau) furniture, Art Deco, and reliquaries.

Cost and Hours: Covered by Kulturforum combo-ticket and Museumspass, Tue-Fri 10:00-18:00, Sat-Sun 11:00-18:00, closed Mon, Herbert-von-Karajan-Strasse 10, tel. 030/266-424-242, www.smb.museum/kgm.

▲Musical Instruments Museum (Musikinstrumenten Museum)

This impressive hall is filled with 600 exhibits spanning the 16th century to modern times. Wander among old keyboard instruments and funny-looking tubas. Pick up the included audioguide and free English brochure at the entry. In addition to the English commentary, the audioguide has clips of various instruments being played (just punch in the number next to the instrument you want to hear). This place is fascinating if you're into pianos.

Cost and Hours: €4, covered by Kulturforum combo-ticket and Museumspass, Tue-Fri 9:00-17:00, Thu until 20:00, Sat-Sun 10:00-17:00, closed Mon, low-profile white building east of the big yellow Philharmonic Concert Hall, tel. 030/2548-1178, www.sim.spk-berlin.de.

Philharmonic Concert Hall

Poke into the lobby of Berlin's yellow Philharmonic building and see if there are tickets available during your stay. The interior is famous for its extraordinary acoustics. Even from the outside, this is a remarkable building, designed by a nautical engineer to look like a ship—notice how different it looks from each angle. Inexpensive and legitimate tickets are often sold on the street before performances. Or you can buy tickets from the box office in person, by phone, or online (ticket office open Mon-Fri 15:00-18:00, Sat-Sun 11:00-14:00, tel. 030/2548-8999—answered daily 9:00-18:00, www.berliner-philharmoniker.de). For guest performances, you must buy tickets through the organizer (see website for details).

Sights in Western Berlin

Throughout the Cold War, Western travelers—and most West Berliners—got used to thinking of western Berlin's Kurfürstendamm boulevard as the heart of the city. But those days have gone the way of the Wall. With the huge changes the city has undergone since 1989, the real "city center" is now, once again, Berlin's historic center (the Mitte district, around Unter den Linden and Friedrichstrasse). While western Berlin still works well as a home base, it's no longer the obvious place from which to explore Berlin. After the new Hauptbahnhof essentially put Bahnhof Zoo out of business in 2006, the area was left with an identity crisis. Now, more than 20 years after reunification, the west side is back and has fully embraced its historical role as a chic, classy suburb.

In the Heart of Western Berlin

A few interesting sights sit within walking distance of Bahnhof Zoo and the Savignyplatz hotels.

▲Kurfürstendamm

Western Berlin's main drag, Kurfürstendamm boulevard (nicknamed "Ku'damm"), starts at Kaiser Wilhelm Memorial Church and does a commercial cancan for two miles. In the 1850s, when Berlin became a wealthy and important capital, her "new rich" chose Kurfürstendamm as their street. Bismarck made it Berlin's Champs-Elysées. In the 1920s, it became a stylish and fashionable drag of cafés and boutiques. During the Third Reich, as home to an international community of diplomats and journalists, it enjoyed more freedom than the rest of Berlin. Throughout the Cold War, economic subsidies from the West made sure that capitalism thrived on Ku'damm. And today, while much of the old charm has been hamburgerized, Ku'damm is still a fine place to enjoy elegant shops (around Fasanenstrasse), department stores, and people-watching.

▲Kaiser Wilhelm Memorial Church (Gedächtniskirche)

This church was originally dedicated to the first emperor of Germany. Reliefs and mosaics show great events in the life of Germany's favorite *Kaiser*, from his coronation in 1871 to his death in 1888. The church's bombed-out ruins have been left standing as a poignant memorial to the destruction of Berlin in World War II.

Cost and Hours: Church—free, daily 9:00-19:00; Memorial Hall—free, Mon-Sat 10:00-18:00, Sun 12:00-17:30. Located on Breitscheidplatz, U2/U9 and S-Bahn: Zoologischer Garten or U1/U9: Kurfürstendamm, www.gedaechtniskirche.com.

Visiting the Church: The church is actually an ensemble of buildings: a new church, the matching bell tower, a meeting hall, and the bombed-out ruins of the old church, with its Memorial Hall. The current renovation project will strengthen the foundations of all four buildings and make it possible for visitors to get to the top of the church for the first time in 60 years.

Under a Neo-Romanesque mosaic ceiling, the **Memorial Hall** features a small exhibit of interesting photos about the bombing and before-and-after models of the church. After the war, some Berliners wanted to tear down the ruins and build it anew. Instead, it was decided to keep what was left of the old church as a memorial and stage a competition to design a contemporary, add-on section. The winning entry—the short, modern church (1961) next to the Memorial Hall—offers a meditative world of 11,000 little blue windows. The blue glass was given to the church by the French as a reconciliation gift. For more information on both churches, pick up the English flier (€0.50).

As you enter the **church,** a peaceful blue oasis in the middle of the busy city, turn immediately right to find a simple charcoal sketch of the Virgin Mary wrapped in a shawl. During the Battle of Stalingrad, German combat surgeon Kurt Reuber rendered the Virgin on the back of a stolen Soviet map to comfort the men in his care. On the right are the words "Light, Life, Love" from the gospel of John; on the left, "Christmas in the cauldron 1942"; and at the bottom, "Fortress Stalingrad." Though Reuber died in captivity a year later, his sketch was flown out of Stalingrad on the last medical evacuation flight, and postwar Germany embraced it as a symbol of the wish for peace. Copies of the drawing, now known as the *Stalingrad Madonna,* hang in the Berlin Cathedral, in England's Coventry, and in Russia's Volgograd (formerly Stalingrad) as a sign of peaceful understanding among nations. As another act of reconciliation, every Friday at 13:00 a "Prayers for Peace" service is held simultaneously with the cathedral in Coventry.

Nearby: The lively square between the churches and the Europa Center (a once-impressive, shiny high-rise shopping center built as a showcase of Western capitalism during the Cold War) usually attracts street musicians and performers—especially in the summer. Berliners call the funky fountain the "wet meatball."

The Story of Berlin

Filling most of what seems like a department store right on Ku'damm (at #207), this sprawling history exhibit tells the stormy 800-year story of Berlin in a creative way. While there are almost no real historic artifacts, the exhibit does a good job of cobbling together many dimensions of the life and tumultuous times of this great city. It's particularly strong on the story of the city from World War I through the Cold War. However, for similar information, and more artifacts, the German History Museum on Unter den Linden is a far better use of your time and money.

Cost and Hours: €12, discount with WelcomeCard, daily 10:00-20:00, last entry 2 hours before closing, tel. 030/8872-0100, www.story-of-berlin.de. Times for the 30-minute bunker tour are posted at the entry.

▲Käthe Kollwitz Museum

This local artist (1867-1945), who experienced much of Berlin's stormiest century, conveys some powerful, deeply felt emotions about motherhood, war, and suffering through the stark faces of her art. This small yet fine collection (the only one in town of Kollwitz's work) consists of three floors of charcoal drawings, topped by an attic with a handful of sculptures.

Cost and Hours: €6, daily 11:00-18:00, a block off Ku'damm at Fasanenstrasse 24, U-Bahn: Uhlandstrasse, tel. 030/882-5210, www.kaethe-kollwitz.de.

▲Kaufhaus des Westens (KaDeWe)

The "Department Store of the West" has been a Berlin tradition for more than a century. With a staff of 2,100 to help you sort through its vast selection of 380,000 items, KaDeWe claims to be the biggest department store on the Continent. You can get everything from a haircut and train ticket (third floor) to souvenirs (fourth floor). The theater and concert box office on the sixth floor charges an 18 percent booking fee, but they know all your options (cash only). The sixth floor is a world of gourmet taste treats. The biggest selection of deli and exotic food in Germany offers plenty of classy opportunities to sit down and eat. Ride the glass elevator to the seventh floor's glass-domed Winter Garden, a self-service cafeteria—fun but pricey.

Hours: Mon-Thu 10:00-20:00, Fri 10:00-21:00, Sat 9:30-20:00, closed Sun, S-Bahn: Zoologischer Garten or U-Bahn: Wittenbergplatz, tel. 030/21210, www.kadewe.de.

Nearby: The Wittenbergplatz U-Bahn station (in front of KaDeWe) is a unique opportunity to see an old-time station. Enjoy its interior with classic advertisements still decorating its venerable walls.

Berlin Zoo and Aquarium (Zoologischer Garten Berlin)

More than 1,500 different kinds of animals call Berlin's famous zoo home...or so the zookeepers like to think. The big hit here is the lonely panda bear (straight in from the entrance). The adjacent aquarium is world-class.

Cost and Hours: Zoo-€13, aquarium-€13, €20 for both, kids half-price, discount with WelcomeCard, daily 9:00-18:00, aquarium closes 30 minutes earlier; feeding times—*Fütterungszeiten*—posted just inside entrance, the best feeding show is the sea lions—generally at 15:15; enter near Europa Center in front of Hotel Palace or opposite Bahnhof Zoo on Hardenbergplatz, Budapester Strasse 34, tel. 030/254-010, www.zoo-berlin.de.

Erotic Art Museum (Erotikmuseum)

This offers two floors of graphic art (especially East Asian), old-time sex-toy knickknacks, and a special exhibit on the queen of German pornography, the late Beate Uhse. This amazing woman, a former test pilot for the Third Reich and groundbreaking purveyor of condoms and sex ed in the 1950s, was the female Hugh Hefner of Germany and CEO of a huge chain of porn shops. She is famously credited with bringing sex out of the bedroom...and onto the kitchen table ("where it belongs," adds my Berliner friend). FYI: You'll see much more sex for half the price in a private video booth next door.

Cost and Hours: €9, Mon-Wed 9:00-22:00, Thu-Sat 9:00-23:30, Sun 11:00-22:00, hard-to-beat gift shop, at corner of Kantstrasse and Joachimstalerstrasse, a block from Bahnhof Zoo, tel. 030/886-0666, http://erotikmuseum.beate-uhse.com.

Charlottenburg Palace Area

The Charlottenburg district—with a cluster of museums across the street from a grand palace—is an easy side-trip from downtown. The palace isn't much to see, but if the surrounding museums appeal to you, consider making the trip.

Getting There: Ride U2 to Sophie-Charlotte Platz and walk 10 minutes up the tree-lined boulevard Schlossstrasse (following signs

BERLIN

Charlottenburg Palace Area

to *Schloss*), or—much faster—catch bus #M45 (direction Spandau) direct from Bahnhof Zoo.

Eating near Charlottenburg Palace: For a Charlottenburg lunch, the **Brauhaus Lemke** is a comfortable brewpub restaurant with a copper and woody atmosphere, good local microbeers (*dunkles* means "dark," *helles* is "light"), and traditional German grub (€8-17 meals, daily 11:00-24:00, fun for groups, across from palace at Luisenplatz 1, tel. 030/3087-8979). Or consider lunching like the Russians, who have been part of Charlottenburg ever since Frederick the Great invited them in the 18th century. The small **Samovar** serves traditional Russian specialties in a comfortable, intimate setting (€6-23 meals, daily 11:00-22:00, just past Brauhaus Lemke at Luisenplatz 3, tel. 030/341-4154).

▲Charlottenburg Palace (Schloss Charlottenburg)

If you've seen the great palaces of Europe, this Baroque palace, also known as the Altes Schloss, comes in at about number 10 (behind Potsdam, too). It's the largest former residence of the royal Hohenzollern family in Berlin and contains the biggest collection of 17th-century French fresco painting outside France. The **Neue Flügel** (a.k.a. the Knobelsdorff Wing) has a separate entry fee and features a few royal apartments. Go upstairs and take a substantial hike through restored-since-the-war gold-crusted white rooms.

Cost and Hours: Palace-€12, includes audioguide, Tue-Sun 10:00-18:00, until 17:00 Nov-March, closed Mon, last entry 30 minutes before closing, tel. 030/320-911; Neue Flügel-€6, more during special exhibitions, includes audioguide, Wed-Mon 10:00-

17:00, closed Tue, last entry at 16:30, when facing the palace walk toward the right wing, tel. 0331/969-4200, then press 1, www. spsg.de. The only WC is within the castle, mid-tour.

▲Museum Berggruen

This tidy little museum is a pleasant surprise. Climb three floors through a fun and substantial collection of Picassos. Along the way, you'll see plenty of notable works by Henri Matisse, Paul Klee, and Alberto Giacometti.

Cost and Hours: €10 combo-ticket includes the Scharf-Gerstenberg Collection—described later, covered by Museumspass, open Tue-Sun 10:00-18:00, closed Mon, Schlossstrasse 1, tel. 030/326-95815, www.smb.museum.

▲Bröhan Museum

Wander through a dozen beautifully furnished *Jugendstil* and Art Deco living rooms, a curvy organic world of lamps, glass, silver, and posters. English descriptions are posted on the wall of each room on the main floor. While you're there, look for the fine collection of Impressionist paintings by Karl Hagemeister.

Cost and Hours: €6, Museumspass doesn't cover special exhibits, Tue-Sun 10:00-18:00, closed Mon, Schlossstrasse 1A, tel. 030/3269-0600, www.broehan-museum.de.

▲Scharf-Gersternberg Collection

This small museum houses a collection of more than 250 works of Surrealist and pre-Surrealist art. The *Surreal Worlds* exhibit shows just how freaky the world looked to artists like Salvador Dalí, Paul Klee, and Francisco de Goya. Be sure to check out Dalí's film of his birth from an egg on the beach.

Cost and Hours: €10 combo-ticket includes Museum Berggruen—described earlier, open Tue-Sun 10:00-18:00, closed Mon, Schlossstrasse 70, tel. 030/3435-7315, www.smb.museum.

Nightlife in Berlin

Berlin is a happening place for nightlife—whether it's clubs, pubs, jazz music, cabaret, hokey-but-fun German variety shows, theater, or concerts.

Entertainment Info: *Berlin Programm* lists a nonstop parade of concerts, plays, exhibits, and cultural events (€2, in German, www.berlin-programm.de); *Exberliner Magazine* (€3, www.exberliner.com) doesn't have as much hard information, but is colorfully written in English (both sold at kiosks and TIs). For the young and determined sophisticate, *Zitty* and *Tip* are the top guides to alternative culture (in German, sold at kiosks). Also pick up the free schedules *Flyer* and *030* in bars and clubs. Visit KaDeWe's ticket office for your music and theater options (sixth floor, 18 percent fee but access to all tickets). Ask about "competitive improvisation" and variety shows.

Half-Price Tickets: Hekticket, Berlin's ticket clearinghouse, is good for whatever's happening in town. They offer regular tickets in advance and same-day half-price tickets to concerts, cabaret, theater, and so on. Drop by or call after 14:00 to see what's on the push list for this evening—ticket prices usually range from €10 to €20 (Mon-Sat 12:00-20:00, closed Sun, half-price sales start at 14:00, Karl-Liebknecht-Strasse 13, tel. 030/230-9930, www.hekticket.de). They also have a branch in western Berlin (near Bahnhof Zoo, across from Kaiser Wilhelm Memorial Church, at Hardenbergstrasse 29).

Berlin Jazz

To enjoy live music near my recommended Savignyplatz hotels in western Berlin, consider **A Trane Jazz Club** (all jazz, great stage and intimate seating, €7-18 cover depending on act, opens at 21:00, live music nightly 22:00-2:00 in the morning, Bleibtreustrasse 1, tel. 030/313-2550, www.a-trane.de). **B-Flat Acoustic Music and Jazz Club,** in the heart of eastern Berlin, also has live music nightly—and shares a courtyard with a tranquil tea house (shows vary from free to €10-12 cover, open Sun-Thu from 20:00 with shows starting at 21:00, Fri-Sat from 21:00 with shows at 22:00, a block from Rosenthaler Platz U-Bahn stop at Rosenthaler Strasse 13, tel. 030/283-3123, www.b-flat-berlin.de).

Berliner Rock and Roll

Berlin has a vibrant rock and pop scene, with popular venues at the Spandau Citadel and the outdoor Waldbühne ("Forest Stage"). Check out what's playing on posters in the U-Bahn, in *Zitty*, or at any ticket agency. Great Berlin bands include The Beatsteaks (punk rock), Jennifer Rostock (punk rock), and Seeed (funky ska).

Cabaret

Bar Jeder Vernunft offers modern-day cabaret a short walk from my recommended hotels in western Berlin. This variety show—under a classic old tent perched atop the modern parking lot of the Berliner Festspiele theater—is a hit with German speakers, and can be worthwhile for those who don't speak the language (as some of the music shows are in a sort of *Deutsch*-English hybrid). Some Americans even perform here periodically. Tickets run about €22-25, and shows change regularly (performances generally start Tue-Sat at 20:00, Sun at 19:00, seating can be a bit cramped, south of Ku'damm at Schaperstrasse 24, U3 or U9: Spichernstrasse, tel. 030/883-1582, www.bar-jeder-vernunft.de).

German Variety Show

To spend an evening enjoying Europe's largest revue theater, consider the long-running "Show Me" at the **FriedrichstadtPalast.** It's a lavish visual spectacle, alternating between gentle, poetic interludes and vivid dance numbers (€17-105, no shows Mon or Wed, Friedrichstrasse 107, U6: Oranienburger Tor, tel. 030/2326-2326, www.show-palace.eu).

Nightclubs and Pubs

Oranienburger Strasse is a trendy scene, with bars and restaurants spilling out onto sidewalks filled with people strolling. To the north, you'll find the hip Prenzlauer Berg neighborhood, packed with everything from smoky pubs to small art bars and dance clubs (best scene is around Helmholtzplatz, U2: Eberswalder Strasse).

Dancing

Cut a rug at **Clärchens Ballhaus,** an old ballroom that's been a Berlin institution since 1913. At some point everyone in Berlin comes through here, as the dance hall attracts an eclectic Berlin-in-a-nutshell crowd of grannies, elegant women in evening dresses, yuppies, scensters, and hippies. The music (swing, waltz, tango, or cha-cha) changes every day, with live music on Friday and Saturday (from 23:15, €4 cover; dance hall open daily from 10:00—12:00 in winter—until the last person goes home, in the heart of the Auguststrasse gallery district at Auguststrasse 24, S-Bahn: Oranienburger Strasse, tel. 030/282-9295, www.ballhaus.de). Dancing lessons are also available (€8, Mon-Tue at 19:00, Thu at 19:30, 1.5 hours). The "Gypsy" restaurant, which fills a huge courtyard out front, serves decent food and good pizza.

Art Galleries

Berlin, a magnet for new artists, is a great city for gallery visits. Galleries—many of which stay open late—welcome visitors who are "just looking." The most famous gallery district is in eastern Berlin's Mitte neighborhood, along **Auguststrasse** (branches off from Oranienburger Strasse). Check out the Berlin outpost of the edgy-yet-accessible art of the New Leipzig movement at **Galerie Eigen+Art** (Tue-Sat 11:00-18:00, closed Sun-Mon, Auguststrasse 26, tel. 030/280-6605, www.eigen-art.com). The other gallery area is in western Berlin, along **Fasanenstrasse.**

Pub Crawls

The "free" tour companies that cater to students offer wildly popular pub crawls, promising "four cool bars and one hot club" for €12. Just imagine what kind of bar lets in a tour of 70 college kids. It can be fun...if you want to get drunk with a bunch of American students in a foreign country.

Sleeping in Berlin

When in Berlin, I used to sleep in the former West, on or near Savignyplatz—and I still list good options there. But these days, the focus of Berlin is in the East, and I've recommended places in the colorful Prenzlauer Berg district.

Berlin is packed and hotel prices go up on holidays, including Green Week in mid-January, Easter weekend, the first weekend in May, Ascension weekend in May, German Unity Day (Oct 3), Christmas, and New Year's.

In Eastern Berlin

Prenzlauer Berg

If you want to sleep in the former East Berlin, set your sights on the colorful and gritty Prenzlauer Berg district. After decades of neglect, this corner of eastern Berlin has quickly come back to life. Gentrification has brought Prenzlauer Berg great hotels, tasty ethnic and German eateries (see "Eating in Berlin," later), and a happening nightlife scene. Think of all the graffiti as just some people's way of saying they care. The huge and impersonal concrete buildings are enlivened with a street fair of fun little shops and eateries.

This loosely defined area is about 1.5 miles north of Alexanderplatz, roughly between Kollwitzplatz and Helmholtzplatz, and to the west, along Kastanienallee (known affectionately as "Casting Alley" for its generous share of beautiful people). The closest U-Bahn stops are U2: Senefelderplatz at the south end of the neighborhood, U8: Rosenthaler Platz in the middle, or U2: Eberswalder Strasse at the north end. Or, for less walking, take the S-Bahn to Hackescher Markt, then catch tram #M1 north.

$$$ Precise Hotel Myer's Berlin rents 60 simple, small rooms. The gorgeous public spaces include a patio and garden. This peaceful hub—off a quiet garden courtyard and tree-lined street, just a five-minute walk from Kollwitzplatz or the nearest U-Bahn stop (Senefelderplatz)—makes it hard to believe you're in a capital city. Their five classes of rooms range from three to five stars, hence the wide price range (Sb-€80-195, Db-€108-235, price also depends on season—check rates online for your dates, air-con in some rooms, elevator, guest computer, free Wi-Fi, Metzer Strasse 26, tel. 030/440-140, www.myershotel.de, info@myershotel.com).

$$$ Hotel Jurine (zhoo-REEN—the family name) is a pleasant 53-room business-style hotel whose friendly staff aims to please. In good weather, you can enjoy the breakfast buffet on the peaceful backyard patio and garden (Sb-€90-110, Db-€130-160, extra bed-€35, rates vary by season, check their website for discounts July-Aug, mention this book to get courtyard-facing room at no extra charge if one's available, elevator, free Wi-Fi, parking

---

Sleep Code

(€1 = about $1.30, country code: 49, area code: 030)
S = Single, **D** = Double/Twin, **T** = Triple, **Q** = Quad, **b** = bathroom, **s** = shower only. Unless otherwise noted, credit cards are accepted, English is spoken, and breakfast is included.

To help you sort easily through these listings, I've divided the accommodations into three categories, based on the price for a standard double room with bath:

$$$ Higher Priced—Most rooms €125 or more.
$$ Moderately Priced—Most rooms between €85-125.
$ Lower Priced—Most rooms €85 or less.

Prices can change without notice; verify the hotel's current rates online or by email. For the best prices, always book direct.

---

garage-€13.50—reserve ahead, Schwedter Strasse 15, 10-minute walk to U2: Senefelderplatz, tel. 030/443-2990, www.hotel-jurine.de, mail@hotel-jurine.de).

$$ Hotel Kastanienhof feels less urban-classy and more like a traditional small-town German hotel. It's wonderfully located on the Kastanienallee #M1 tram line, with easy access to the Prenzlauer Berg bustle. Its 42 slightly overpriced rooms come with helpful service (Sb-€74-94, Db-€105-140, extra bed-€29, reception closed 22:00-6:30—call ahead to make arrangements to get key if you'll arrive late, elevator, free cable Internet in rooms, Wi-Fi in lobby, parking-€9/day, 20 yards from #M1 Zionskirche tram stop at Kastanienallee 65, tel. 030/443-050, www.kastanienhof.biz, info@kastanienhof.biz).

$$ The Circus Hotel, run by the popular hostel listed later, caters to youth hostelers who've outgrown the backpacker lifestyle. Each of its 60 colorful, trendy rooms has a unique bit of decoration. It overlooks a busy intersection, so there's some nighttime noise—try asking for a quieter back room. Owing to its idealistic youth-hostel roots, it's very service-oriented, with lots of included extras, a very "green" attitude, and occasional special events for guests (Sb-€70, small standard Db-€80, larger Db-€90, junior suite Db-€100, breakfast-€4-8, elevator, guest computer, free Wi-Fi, mellow ground-floor restaurant, Rosenthaler Strasse 1, directly at U8: Rosenthaler Platz, tel. 030/2000-3939, www.circus-berlin.de, info@circus-berlin.de). The Circus also offers a range of spacious, modern **apartments** two blocks away on Choriner Strasse (Db-€130-€250 depending on size and furnishings, 3-night minimum stay preferred).

BERLIN

Eastern Berlin Accommodations

1. Precise Hotel Myer's Berlin
2. Hotel Jurine
3. Hotel Kastanienhof
4. The Circus Hotel
5. Karlito Apartmenthaus
6. easyHotel Berlin Hackescher Markt
7. Hotel Augustinenhof
8. Circus Hostel & Internet Café
9. Meininger Hotels (3)
10. EastSeven Hostel
11. Hotel Transit Loft
12. To Ostel
13. Bike Rentals (2)

BERLIN

$ Karlito Apartmenthaus offers 12 well-located, modern, and comfortable apartments above a hip café on a tranquil side street near Hackescher Markt. All of the sleek, Ikea-esque units have miniature balconies and are fully equipped (Sb-€62-77, Db-€72-85, price depends on season, extra person-€15, up to 2 children under 8 sleep free with 2 paying adults, breakfast in Café Lois-€5, no minimum stay, elevator, free Wi-Fi, bike rental-€8/day, Linienstrasse 60—check in at Café Lois around the corner on Gormannstrasse, 350 yards from S-Bahn: Hackescher Markt, even closer to U8: Rosenthaler Platz, mobile 0179-704-9041, www.karlito-apartments.de, info@karlito-apartments.de).

$ easyHotel Berlin Hackescher Markt is part of an unapologetically cheap Europe-wide chain where you pay for exactly what you use—nothing more, nothing less. Based on parent company easyJet's sales model of nickel-and-dime air travel, the hotel has inexpensive base rates (small Db-€25-65, larger Db-€35-65, prices vary by season, it's cheaper to book earlier), then charges you separately for optional extras (breakfast, Wi-Fi, using the TV, and so on). The 125 orange-and-gray rooms are very small, basic, and feel popped out of a plastic mold, but if you skip the extras, the price is right, and the location—at the Hackescher Markt end of Prenzlauer Berg—is wonderful (air-con, elevator, after booking online call to request a quieter back room, Rosenthaler Strasse 69, tel. 030/4000-6550, www.easyhotel.com).

Near Oranienburger Strasse: **$$$ Hotel Augustinenhof** is a clean hotel with 66 spacious rooms, nice woody floors, and some of the most comfortable beds in Berlin. While not exactly in Prenzlauer Berg, the hotel is on a side street near all the Oranienburger Strasse action. Rooms in front overlook the courtyard of the old Imperial Post Office, rooms in back are a bit quieter, and all rooms have old, thin windows (official rates: Sb-€119, Db-€151—but you'll likely pay closer to Db-€100, elevator, free Wi-Fi or cable Internet in rooms, Auguststrasse 82, 50 yards from S-Bahn: Oranienburger Strasse, tel. 030/308-860, www.hotel-augustinenhof.de, augustinenhof@albrechtshof-hotels.de).

Hostels in Eastern Berlin

Berlin is known among budget travelers for its fun, hip hostels. These range from upscale-feeling hostels with some hotelesque private rooms comfortable enough even for non-hostelers, to more truly backpacker-type places where comfort is secondary to socializing. These are scattered around eastern Berlin, including some (Circus, Meininger, and EastSeven) in the Prenzlauer Berg area just described.

Comfortable Hostels with Hotelesque Rooms

$ Circus is a brightly colored, well-run place with 230 beds, a trendy lounge with upscale ambience, and a bar downstairs. It has typical hostel dorms as well as some very hotel-like private rooms; for a step up in quality, see the listing for the Circus Hotel, earlier (€23/bed in 8- to 10-bed dorms, €27/bed in 4- to 5-bed dorms, S-€50, Sb-€60, D-€66, Db-€85, Tb-€95, 2-person apartment with kitchen-€100, 4-person apartment-€160, breakfast-€4-8, no curfew, elevator, pay guest computer, free Wi-Fi, bike rental, Weinbergsweg 1A, U8: Rosenthaler Platz, tel. 030/2000-3939, www.circus-berlin.de, info@circus-berlin.de).

$ Meininger is a Europe-wide budget-hotel chain with several locations in Berlin. With sleek, nicely decorated rooms, these are a great-value budget option, even for non-hostelers. They have three particularly appealing branches: in Prenzlauer Berg (Schönhauser Allee 19 on Senefelderplatz), at Oranienburger Strasse 67 (next to the Aufsturz pub), and near the Hauptbahnhof, at Ella-Traebe-Strasse 9 (rates vary by availability, but usually €20-22/bed in 6-bed dorms, Sb-€52, Db-€70, Tb-€86; rates at Hauptbahnhof location about €5-10 more; all locations: breakfast-€5.50, elevator, 24-hour reception, pay guest computer, free Wi-Fi in lobby, tel. 030/666-36100, www.meininger-hostels.de).

Backpacker Havens

$ EastSeven Hostel rents the best cheap beds in Prenzlauer Berg. It's sleek and modern, with all the hostel services and more: 60 beds, inviting lounge, fully equipped guest kitchen, lockers, quiet backyard terrace, and bike rental. Children are welcome. Easygoing people of any age are comfortable here (€18/bed in 8-bed dorms, €22/bed in 4-bed dorms with private bathroom—or €20/bed in dorm with bathroom down the hall, S-€38, D-€52, T-€66, private rooms have bathrooms down the hall, includes sheets, towel-€1, continental breakfast-€2, guest computer, free Wi-Fi, laundry-€5, no curfew, 100 yards from U2: Senefelderplatz at Schwedter Strasse 7, tel. 030/9362-2240, www.eastseven.de, info@eastseven.de).

$ Hotel Transit Loft, actually a hostel, is located in a refurbished factory. Its 62 clean, high-ceilinged, modern rooms and wide-open lobby have an industrial touch. The reception—staffed by friendly, hip Berliners—is open 24 hours, with a bar serving drinks all night long (€21/bed in 4- to 6-bed dorms, Sb-€59, Db-€69, Tb-€89, includes sheets and breakfast, elevator, pay guest computer, free Wi-Fi, fully wheelchair-accessible, down alley facing inner courtyard at Immanuelkirchstrasse 14A; U2/U5/U8 or S-Bahn: Alexanderplatz, then tram #M4 to Hufelandstrasse and walk 50 yards; tel. 030/4849-3773, www.transit-loft.de, loft@hotel-transit.de).

$ Ostel is a fun retro-1970s-DDR apartment building that re-creates the lifestyle and interior design of a country relegated to the dustbin of history. All the furniture and room decorations have been meticulously collected and restored to their former socialist glory—only the psychedelic wallpaper is a replica. Guests buy ration vouchers (€7.50/person) for breakfast in the attached restaurant. Kitschy, sure—but also clean and memorable (€15/bed in a 4- or 6-bed "Pioneer Camp" room or in 12-bunk dorm—includes lockers, S-€33, Sb-€40, D-€54, Db-€64, 4-person apartments-€120, includes sheets and towels, 24-hour reception, free Wi-Fi in lobby, bike rental, free parking, free collective use of the people's barbeque, right behind Ostbahnhof station on the corner of Strasse der Pariser Kommune at Wriezener Karree 5, tel. 030/2576-8660, www.ostel.eu, contact@ostel.eu).

In Western Berlin
Near Savignyplatz and Bahnhof Zoo
While Bahnhof Zoo and Ku'damm are no longer the center of the action, this western Berlin neighborhood is still a comfortable and handy home base (thanks to its easy transit connections to the rest of the city). The streets around the tree-lined Savignyplatz (a 10-minute walk behind the station) have a neighborhood charm, with an abundance of simple, small, friendly, good-value places to sleep and eat. The area has an artsy aura going back to the cabaret days in the 1920s, when it was the center of Berlin's gay scene. The hotels and pensions I list here—which are all a 5- to 15-minute walk from Bahnhof Zoo and Savignyplatz (with S- and U-Bahn stations)—are generally located a couple of flights up in big, run-down buildings. Inside, they're clean and spacious enough so that their well-worn character is actually charming. Asking for a quieter room in back gets you away from any street noise. Of the accommodations listed here, Pension Peters offers the best value for budget travelers.

$$ Hecker's Hotel is a modern, four-star hotel with 69 big, fresh rooms and all the Euro-comforts. Their "superior" rooms cost €10 more than their "comfort" rooms, and—while the same size—have more modern furnishings and air-conditioning. Herr Kiesel promises free breakfasts (otherwise €16/person) for Rick Steves readers booking direct via the hotel's website or email (Sb-€85, Db-usually €95-100—though all rooms €180 during conferences, generally €100 July-Aug, look for deals on their website, non-smoking rooms, elevator, free Wi-Fi, parking-€14-20/day, between Savignyplatz and Ku'damm at Grolmanstrasse 35, tel. 030/88900, www.heckers-hotel.com, info@heckers-hotel.com).

$$ Hotel Askanischerhof, the oldest B&B in Berlin, is posh as can be, with 16 sprawling, antique-furnished living rooms you can call home. Photos on the walls brag of famous movie-star guests. It oozes Old World service and classic Berlin atmosphere (Sb-€110, Db-€120, Tb-€130, elevator, free Wi-Fi, parking-€4/day, Ku'damm 53, tel. 030/881-8033, www.askanischer-hof.de, info@askanischer-hof.de).

$$ Hotel Astoria is a friendly three-star business-class hotel with 32 comfortably furnished rooms and affordable summer and weekend rates (Sb-€60, Db-€108-126, often Db-€80 in summer, check their website for deals, non-smoking floors, breakfast-€10, elevator, guest computer, free Wi-Fi, bike rental, parking-€9/day, around corner from Bahnhof Zoo at Fasanenstrasse 2, tel. 030/312-4067, www.hotelastoria.de, info@hotelastoria.de).

$$ Hotel Carmer 16, with 34 bright and airy (if a bit dated) rooms, is both business-like and homey, and has an inviting lounge and charming balconies (Sb-€78, Db-€105, Qb-€154, extra person-€30, some rooms have balconies, family suites, elevator and a few stairs, free Wi-Fi, parking €9.50/day, Carmerstrasse 16, tel. 030/3110-0500, www.hotel-carmer16.de, info@hotel-carmer16.de).

$$ Hotel-Pension Funk, the former home of a 1920s silent-movie star, is a delightfully quirky time warp. Kind manager Herr Michael Pfundt offers 15 elegant old rooms with rich Art Nouveau furnishings (S-€42, Ss-€60, Sb-€72, D-€72, Ds-€85, Db-€99, extra person-€25, cash preferred, free Wi-Fi, a long block south of Ku'damm at Fasanenstrasse 69, tel. 030/882-7193, www.hotel-pensionfunk.de, berlin@hotel-pensionfunk.de).

$$ Hotel Bogota is a slumbermill just steps off Ku'damm, renting 115 rooms in a sprawling maze of a building that used to house the Nazi Chamber of Culture. A creaky, well-worn place with big, simple rooms and old furniture, it has the feel of a once-grand hotel (S-€49, Ss-€62, Sb-€98, D-€77, Ds-€84, Db-€89-150, extra bed-€21, check their website for deals and great last-minute prices in summer, children under 14 free, elevator, guest computer, free Wi-Fi, little back garden, 10-minute walk from Savignyplatz at Schlüterstrasse 45, tel. 030/881-5001, www.hotel-bogota.de, info@hotel-bogota.de).

$ Pension Peters, run by a German-Swedish couple, is sunny and central, with a cheery breakfast room and a super-friendly staff who go out of their way to help their guests. With its sleek Scandinavian decor and 34 renovated rooms, it's a good choice. Some of the ground-floor rooms facing the back courtyard are a bit dark—and cheaper for the inconvenience (Sb-€58, Db-€79, big Db-€85, extra bed-€15, family room-€85, these special prices offered only with this book in 2014—mention when you reserve, up to 2 kids under 13 free with 2 paying adults, cash preferred, organic breakfast, guest computer, free Wi-Fi, bike rental, 10 yards off Savignyplatz

Western Berlin

❶ Hecker's Hotel
❷ Hotel Askanischerhof
❸ Hotel Astoria
❹ Hotel Carmer 16
❺ Hotel-Pension Funk
❻ Hotel Bogota
❼ Pension Peters
❽ Restaurant Marjellchen
❾ Rest. Leibniz-Klause
❿ Dicke Wirtin Pub
⓫ To Weyers Restaurant
⓬ Café Literaturhaus
⓭ Die Zwölf Apostel Rest.
⓮ Zillemarkt Restaurant
⓯ Technische Universität Mensa
⓰ Ullrich Supermarkt
⓱ Schleusenkrug Beer Garden
⓲ Winter Garden Buffet
⓳ A Trane Jazz Club
⓴ Bar Jeder Vernunft
㉑ Fat Tire Bikes

at Kantstrasse 146, tel. 030/312-2278, www.pension-peters-berlin.de, info@pension-peters-berlin.de, Annika and Christoph with help from his sister, Daisy).

Eating in Berlin

There's a world of restaurants to choose from in this ever-changing city. Your best approach may be to select a neighborhood and browse until you find something that strikes your fancy, rather than seeking out a particular restaurant.

Don't be too determined to eat "Berlin-style." The city is known only for its mildly spicy sausage and for its street food (*Currywurst* and *Döner Kebab*). Germans—especially Berliners—consider their food old-school; when they go out to eat, they're not usually looking for the "traditional local fare" many travelers are after. Nouveau German is California cuisine with scant memories of wurst, kraut, and pumpernickel. If the kraut is getting the wurst of you, take a break with some international or ethnic offerings—try one of the many Turkish, Italian, pan-Asian, and Balkan restaurants.

Colorful pubs—called *Kneipen*—offer light, quick, and easy meals and the fizzy local beer, *Berliner Weiss*. Ask for it *mit Schuss* for a shot of fruity syrup in your suds.

In Eastern Berlin
Near Unter den Linden
While this government/commercial area is hardly a hotspot for eateries, I've listed a few places handy for your sightseeing, all a short walk from Unter den Linden.

Cheap Eats: **Bier's Curry und Spiesse,** under the tracks at the Friedrichstrasse S-Bahn stop, is a great, greasy, cheap, and generous place for an old-fashioned German hot dog. This is the local favorite near Unter den Linden for €2 *Currywurst.* Experiment with variations (the *Flieschspiess* is excellent) and sauces—and don't hold the fried *Zwiebeln* (onions). You'll munch standing at a counter,

BERLIN

Berliner Street Fare

In Berlin, it's easy to eat cheap, with a glut of *Imbiss* snack stands, bakeries (for sandwiches), and falafel/kebab counters. Train stations have grocery stores, as well as bright and modern fruit-and-sandwich bars.

Sausage stands are everywhere (I've listed a couple of local favorites). Most specialize in **Currywurst,** created in Berlin after World War II, when a fast-food cook got her hands on some curry and Worcestershire sauce from British troops stationed here. It's basically a grilled *Bockwurst*-type pork sausage smothered with curry sauce. *Currywurst* comes either *mit Darm* (with casing) or *ohne Darm* (without casing). If the casing is left on to grill, it gives the sausage a smokier flavor. (*Berliner Art*—"Berlin-style"—means that the sausage is boiled *ohne Darm*, then grilled.) Either way, the grilled sausage is then chopped into small pieces or cut in half (East Berlin style) and topped with sauce. While some places simply use ketchup and sprinkle on some curry powder, real *Currywurst* joints use tomato paste, Worcestershire sauce, and curry. With your wurst comes either a toothpick or small wooden fork; you'll usually get a plate of fries as well, but rarely a roll. You'll see *Currywurst* on the menu at some sit-down restaurants, but local purists say that misses the whole point: You'll pay triple and get a less authentic dish than you would at a street stand under elevated S-Bahn tracks.

Other good street foods to consider are *Döner Kebab* (Turkish-style skewered meat slow-roasted and served in a sandwich) and *Frikadelle* (like a hamburger patty; often called *Bulette* in Berlin).

For a quick, cheap, and tasty local hot dog, find one of the portable human hot-dog stands. Two competing companies, Grillrunner and Grillwalker, outfit their cooks in clever harnesses that let them grill and sell hot dogs under an umbrella.

where the people-watching is great (daily 9:00-5:00 in the morning; from inside the station, take the Friedrichstrasse exit and turn left).

Near the Pergamon Museum: Georgenstrasse, a block behind the Pergamon Museum and under the S-Bahn tracks, is lined with fun eateries filling the arcade of the train trestle—close to the sightseeing action but in business mainly for students from nearby Humboldt University. **Deponie3** is a reliable Berlin *Kneipe* usually filled with students. Garden seating in the back is nice if you don't mind the noise of the S-Bahn passing directly above you. The interior is a cozy, wooden wonderland of a bar with several inviting spaces. They serve basic salads, traditional Berlin dishes, and hearty daily specials (€5-8 breakfasts, €8-13 lunches and dinners, open Mon-Fri from 9:00, Sat-Sun from 10:00, Georgenstrasse 5, tel. 030/2016-5740). For Italian food, a branch of **Die Zwölf Apostel** is nearby (food served until 22:00).

Near the TV Tower: **Käse König am Alex** is a wonderfully old-school eatery that's been serving traditional sauerkraut-type dishes since 1933 to hungry locals (with Prussian forks, flat to fit better into a soldier's mess kit). It's fast, the photo menu makes ordering fun, prices are great, and the waitresses are surly (€5-9 dinner plates, daily, Panoramastrasse 1 under the TV Tower, tel. 030/8561-5220). Nearby, **Brauhaus Mitte** is a fun, tour-group-friendly DDR-era beer hall that makes its own beer and offers a menu of Berliner "specialties" and Bavarian dishes. They have decent salads and serve a four-beer sampler board (daily 12:00-24:00, across from the TV Tower at Karl-Liebknecht-Strasse 13, tel. 030/3087-8989).

In the Heart of Old Berlin's Nikolai Quarter: The *Nikolaiviertel* marks the original medieval settlement of Cölln, which would eventually become Berlin. The area was destroyed during the war but was rebuilt for Berlin's 750th birthday in 1987. The whole area has a cute, cobbled, and characteristic old town feel...Middle Ages meets Socialist Realism. Today, the district is pretty soulless by day but a popular restaurant zone at night. **Bräuhaus Georgbrau** is a thriving beer hall serving homemade suds on a picturesque courtyard overlooking the Spree River. Eat in the lively and woody but mod-feeling interior, or outdoors with fun riverside seating—thriving with German tourists. It's a good place to try one of the few typical Berlin dishes: *Eisbein* (boiled ham hock) with sauerkraut and mashed peas with bacon (€11 with a beer and schnapps). The statue of St. George once stood in the courtyard of Berlin's old castle—until the Nazis deemed it too decadent and not "German" enough, and removed it (€7-14 plates, €18 three-foot-long sampler board with a dozen small glasses of beer, daily 10:00-24:00, 2 blocks south of Berlin Cathedral and across the river at Spreeufer 4, tel. 030/242-4244).

In City Hall: Consider lunching at one of Berlin's many *Kantine*. Located in government offices and larger corporations, *Kantine* offer fast, filling, and cheap lunches, along with a unique opportunity to see Germans at work (though the food can hardly be considered gourmet). There are thousands of *Kantine* in Berlin, but the best is **Die Kantine im Roten Rathaus,** in the basement of City Hall. For less than €4, you can get filling German dishes

BERLIN

Eastern Berlin Eateries & Nightlife

1. Bier's Curry und Spiesse
2. Deponie3 Pub
3. Die Zwölf Apostel
4. Käse König am Alex
5. Brauhaus Mitte & Hekticket Half-Price Tix
6. Bräuhaus Georgbrau
7. Die Kantine im Roten Rathaus
8. Lutter & Wegner Rest.; Augustiner am Gendarmenmarkt
9. Galeries Lafayette Food Circus
10. Fresco Espresso Bar
11. Hasir Turkish Restaurant
12. Weihenstephaner Bavarian Restaurant
13. Oranienburger Strasse Eateries
14. Schwarzwaldstuben Pub
15. Luigi Zuckermann Deli & Transit Restaurant
16. Restaurant Simon
17. Prater Biergarten
18. Zum Schusterjungen Speisegaststätte
19. La Bodeguita del Medio Cuban Bar Restaurant
20. Konnopke's Imbiss
21. Restaurant "Die Schule"
22. Kauf Dich Glücklich
23. Gugelhof Restaurant
24. Metzer Eck Pub
25. Humboldt-Box Café
26. To Café Sibylle

..... Former Course of the Wall

500 Meters

1/2 Mile

27 Bonbonmacherei
   Candy Shop

28 Beth Café

29 Fassbender & Rausch
   Chocolate Shop

30 B-Flat Acoustic
   Music & Jazz Club

31 FriedrichstadtPalast

32 Clärchens Ballhaus

like *Leberkäse* (German-style baloney) or stuffed cabbage (Mon-Fri 11:00-14:00, closed Sat-Sun, Rathausstrasse 15).

Near Gendarmenmarkt

South of Unter den Linden, the twin churches of Gendarmenmarkt seem to be surrounded by people in love with food. The lunch and dinner scene is thriving with upscale restaurants serving good cuisine at highly competitive prices to local professionals. If in need of a quick-yet-classy lunch, stroll around the square and along Charlottenstrasse. For a quick bite, head to the cheap *Currywurst* stand behind the German Cathedral.

Lutter & Wegner Restaurant is well-known for its Austrian cuisine (*Schnitzel* and *Sauerbraten*) and popular with businesspeople. It's dressy, with fun sidewalk seating or a dark and elegant interior (€9-18 starters, €16-24 main dishes, daily 11:00-24:00, Charlottenstrasse 56, tel. 030/202-9540).

Augustiner am Gendarmenmarkt, next door to Lutter & Wegner, lines its sidewalk with trademark Bavarian white-and-blue-checkerboard tablecloths; inside, you'll find a classic Bavarian beer-hall atmosphere. Less pretentious than its neighbor, it offers good beer and affordable Bavarian classics in an equally appealing location (€6-12 light meals, €10-16 bigger meals, daily 10:00-24:00, Charlottenstrasse 55, tel. 030/2045-4020).

Galeries Lafayette Food Circus is a French festival of fun eateries in the basement of the landmark department store. You'll find a good deli and prepared-food stands, dishing up cuisine that's good-quality but not cheap (most options €10-15, cheaper €8-10 sandwiches and savory crepes, Mon-Sat 10:00-20:00, closed Sun, Friedrichstrasse 76-78, U-Bahn: Französische Strasse, tel. 030/209-480).

Near Checkpoint Charlie: **Fresco Espresso Bar** is a touristy joint, handy for made-to-order sandwiches. Israeli-born Sagi makes his own bread daily and piles on the fixins for €4-7. This is a popular stop for walking-tour groups: If you get here when they do, expect a line (Mon-Sat 7:30-18:00, Sun 8:00-18:00, in summer until 20:30, Friedrichstrasse 200, tel. 030/2061-6693).

Between the River and Prenzlauer Berg

All of these eateries are within a 10-minute walk of the Hackescher Markt S-Bahn station, in the area butting up against Prenzlauer Berg.

Near Hackescher Markt

Hasir Turkish Restaurant is your chance to dine with candles, hardwood floors, and happy Berliners savoring meaty Anatolian specialties. As Berlin is the world's largest Turkish city outside of Asia Minor, it's no wonder you can find some good Turkish restaurants here. But while most locals think of Turkish food as fast and cheap, this is a dining experience. The restaurant, in a courtyard next to the Hackesche Höfe shopping complex, offers indoor and outdoor tables filled with an enthusiastic local crowd. The service can be a bit questionable, so bring some patience (€6-10 starters, €14-20 main dishes, large and splittable portions, daily 12:00-24:00, in late evening the courtyard is dominated by an unpleasantly loud underground disco, a block from the Hackescher Markt S-Bahn station at Oranienburger Strasse 4, tel. 030/2804-1616).

Weihenstephaner Bavarian Restaurant serves upmarket Bavarian traditional food for around €10-15 a plate; offers an atmospheric cellar, an inner courtyard, and a busy people-watching streetside terrace; and, of course, has excellent beer (daily 11:00-23:00, Neue Promenade 5 at Hackescher Markt, tel. 030/8471-0760).

On or near Oranienburger Strasse

Oranienburger Strasse, a few blocks west of Hackescher Markt, is busy with happy eaters. Restaurants on this stretch come with happy hours and lots of cocktails. **Aufsturz,** a lively pub, has a huge selection of beers and whisky and dishes up "traditional Berliner pub grub" to a young crowd (Oranienburger Strasse 67). **Amrit Lounge** is great on a warm evening if you'd like Indian food outdoors with an umbrellas-in-your-drink Caribbean ambience (€5 cocktails, €10-14 meals, long hours daily, Oranienburger Strasse 44). Next door is **QBA**, a fun Cuban bar and restaurant.

Schwarzwaldstuben, between Oranienburger Strasse and Rosenthaler Platz, is a Black Forest-themed pub—which explains the antlers, cuckoo clocks, and painting of a thick forest on the wall. It's friendly, with good service, food, and prices. The staff chooses the music (often rock or jazz), and the ambience is warm and welcoming. If they're full, you can eat at the long bar or at one of the sidewalk tables (daily 12:00-24:00, Tucholskystrasse 48, tel. 030/2809-8084).

Near Rosenthaler Platz

Surrounding the U8: Rosenthaler Platz station, a short stroll or tram ride from the Hackescher Markt S-Bahn station, and an easy walk from the Oranienburger Strasse action, this busy neighborhood has a few enticing options.

Luigi Zuckermann is a trendy young deli with Israeli/New York style. It's a great spot to pick up a custom-made deli sandwich (choose your ingredients at the deli counter), hummus plate, salad, fresh-squeezed juice, or other quick, healthy lunch. Linger in the interior, grab one of the few sidewalk tables, or take your food to munch on the go (€5-8 meals, daily 8:00-24:00, Rosenthaler Strasse 67, tel. 030/2804-0644).

Transit is a stylish, innovative, affordable Thai/Indonesian/pan-Asian small-plates restaurant. Sit at one of the long shared tables and dig into a creative menu of €3 small plates and €7 big plates. Two people can make a filling meal out of three or four dishes (daily 11:00-late, Rosenthaler Strasse 68, tel. 030/2478-1645).

Restaurant Simon dishes up tasty Italian and German specialties—enjoy them either in the restaurant's simple yet atmospheric interior, or opt for streetside seating (€6-12 main dishes, daily 12:00-22:00, Auguststrasse 53, at intersection with Kleine Auguststrasse, tel. 030/2789-0358).

In Prenzlauer Berg

Prenzlauer Berg is packed with fine restaurants—German, ethnic, and everything in between. Even if you're not staying in this area, it's worth venturing here for dinner. Before making a choice, I'd spend at least a half-hour strolling and browsing through this bohemian wonderland of creative eateries.

Near Eberswalder Strasse

The area surrounding the elevated Eberswalder Strasse U-Bahn station is the epicenter of Prenzlauer Berg—a young, hip, and edgy place to eat and drink. While a bit farther north than other areas I recommend (and a 10- to 15-minute walk from most of my recommended hotels), it's worth the trip to immerse yourself in quintessential Prenzlauer Berg.

Prater Biergarten offers two great eating opportunities: a rustic indoor restaurant and a mellow, shaded, super-cheap, and family-friendly outdoor beer garden (with a playground)—each proudly pouring Prater's own microbrew. In the beer garden—Berlin's oldest—you step up to the counter and order (simple €3-5 plates and an intriguing selection of beer munchies, daily in good weather 12:00-24:00). The restaurant serves serious traditional *Biergarten* cuisine and good salads (€8-19 plates, Mon-Sat 18:00-24:00, Sun 12:00-24:00, cash only, Kastanienallee 7, tel. 030/448-5688).

Zum Schusterjungen Speisegaststätte ("The Cobbler's Apprentice") is a classic old-school, German-with-attitude eatery that retains its circa-1986 DDR decor. Famous for its filling €9-13 meals (including various types of schnitzel and Berlin classics such as pork knuckle), it's a no-frills place with quality ingredients and a strong local following. It serves the eating needs of those Berliners lamenting the disappearance of solid traditional German cooking amid the flood of ethnic eateries (small 40-seat dining hall plus outdoor tables, daily 12:00-24:00, corner of Lychener Strasse and Danziger Strasse 9, tel. 030/442-7654).

La Bodeguita del Medio Cuban Bar Restaurant is purely fun-loving Cuba—graffiti-caked walls, Che Guevara posters, animated staff, and an ambience that makes you want to dance. Come early to eat or late to drink. This restaurant has been here since 1994—and in fast-changing Prenzlauer Berg, that's an eternity. The German-Cuban couple who run it take pride in their food, and the main dishes are big enough to split. You can even puff a Cuban cigar at the sidewalk tables (€4-10 tapas, €7.50 Cuban ribs and salad, Tue-Sun 18:00-24:00, closed Mon, a block from U2: Eberswalder Strasse at Lychener Strasse 6, tel. 030/4050-0601).

Konnopke's Imbiss, a super-cheap German-style sausage stand, has been a Berlin institution for more than 70 years—it was

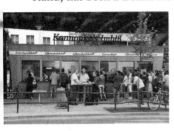

family-owned even during DDR times. Berliners say Konnopke's cooks up some of the city's best *Currywurst* (less than €2). Located beneath the U2 viaduct, the stand was demolished in 2010 during roadwork. Berliners rioted, and Konnopke's was rebuilt in a slick glass-and-steel hut (Mon-Fri 10:00-20:00, Sat 12:00-20:00, closed Sun; Kastanienallee dead-ends at the elevated train tracks, and under them you'll find Konnopke's at Schönhauser Allee 44A, tel. 030/442-7765, www.konnopke-imbiss.de). Don't confuse this with the nearby Currystation—look for the real Konnopke's.

Restaurant "Die Schule" is a modern place with a no-frills style where you can sample traditional German dishes tapas-style. Assemble a collection of little €2.50 plates of old-fashioned German food you might not try otherwise (€9-18 main dishes, good indoor and outdoor seating, daily 11:00-22:00, Kastanienallee 82, tel. 030/780-089-550).

After-Dinner Dessert and Drinks: There are oodles of characteristic funky pubs and nightspots in the area around Helmholtzplatz (and elsewhere in Prenzlauer Berg). Oderberger Strasse is a fun zone to explore. Along here, **Kauf Dich Glücklich** makes a great capper to a Prenzlauer Berg dinner. It serves an enticing array of sweet Belgian waffles and ice cream in a candy-sprinkled, bohemian lounge on a great Prenzlauer Berg street (daily 11:00-24:00 but opens at 10:00 on Sat, indoor and outdoor seating—or get your dessert to go, wait possible on busy nights, Oderberger Strasse 44, tel. 030/4435-2182).

Near Kollwitzplatz

This square, home of the DDR student resistance in 1980s, is now trendy and upscale, popular with hip parents who take their hip kids to the leafy playground park at its center. It's an especially good area to prowl among upmarket restaurants—walk the square and choose. Just about every option offers sidewalk seats in the summer (great on a balmy evening). It's a long block up Kollwitz-strasse from U2: Senefelderplatz.

Gugelhof, right on Kollwitzplatz, is an institution famous for its Alsatian German cuisine. You'll enjoy French quality with German proportions. It's highly regarded, with a boisterous and enthusiastic local crowd filling its minimalist yet classy interior. In good weather, outdoor seating sprawls along its sidewalk. Their fixed-price meals are fun, and they welcome swapping (€20-30 three-course meal, €5-10 starters, €13-22 main dishes, Mon-Fri 16:00-23:30, Sat-Sun 10:00-23:30, reservations required during peak times, where Knaackstrasse meets Kollwitzplatz, tel. 030/442-9229, www.gugelhof.de).

Metzer Eck is a time-warp *Kneipe* with cozy charm and a family tradition dating to 1913. It serves cheap, basic, typical Berlin food with five beers on tap, including the Czech Budvar (€5-9 meals, Mon-Fri 16:00-24:00, Sat 18:00-24:00, closed Sun, Metzer Strasse 33, on the corner with Strassburger Strasse, tel. 030/442-7656).

In Western Berlin

Near Savignyplatz

Many good restaurants are on or within 100 yards of Savignyplatz, near my recommended western Berlin hotels. Savignyplatz is lined with attractive, relaxed, mostly Mediterranean-style places. Take a walk and survey these; continue your stroll along Bleibtreustrasse to discover many trendier, more creative little eateries.

Restaurant Marjellchen is a trip to East Prussia. Dine in a soft, jazzy elegance in one of two six-table rooms. While it doesn't have to be expensive (€10-18 main courses, €27 two-course meals), plan to go the whole nine yards here, as this can be a great experience with caring service. The menu is inviting, and the place family-run—all the recipes were brought to Berlin by the owner's mother after she was expelled from East Prussia. Reservations are smart (daily 17:00-23:30, Mommsenstrasse 9, tel. 030/883-2676, www.marjellchen-berlin.de).

Restaurant Leibniz-Klause is a good place for a dressy German meal. You'll enjoy upscale presentation on white tablecloths, hunter-sized portions, service that's both friendly and professional, and no pretense. Their *Berliner Riesen-Eisbein* ("super pork-leg on the bone"), with sauerkraut and horseradish, will stir even the tiniest amount of Teutonic blood in your veins (€11-22 plates, good indoor and outdoor seating, daily 12:00-late, Leibnizstrasse near corner with Mommsenstrasse, tel. 030/323-7068, www.leibniz-klause.de).

Dicke Wirtin is a pub with traditional old-Berlin *Kneipe* atmosphere, six good beers on tap, and solid home cooking at reasonable prices—such as their famously cheap *Gulaschsuppe* (€4). Their interior is fun and pubby, with soccer on the TV; their streetside tables are also inviting. Pickled eggs are on the bar—ask about how these can help you avoid a hangover (€5 daily specials, €6-16 main dishes, Bavarian Andechs beer on tap, open daily from 12:00, dinner served from 18:00, just off Savignyplatz at Carmerstrasse 9, tel. 030/312-4952).

Weyers offers modern German cuisine in a simple, elegant setting, with dining tables in the summer spilling out into the idyllic neighborhood park in front (€5-10 starters, €10-16 main plates, daily 8:00-24:00, facing Ludwigkirchplatz at corner of Pariser Strasse and Pfalzburger Strasse, tel. 030/881-9378).

Café Literaturhaus is a neighborhood favorite for a light meal, sandwich, or dessert. It has the ambience of an Old World villa with a big garden perfect for their evening poetry readings (€5-15 meals, daily 9:30-24:00, Fasanenstrasse 23, tel. 030/882-5414).

Die Zwölf Apostel ("The Twelve Apostles") is popular for good Italian food. Choose between indoors with candlelit ambience, outdoors on a sun-dappled patio, or overlooking the people parade on its pedestrian street. A local crowd packs this restaurant for €12 pizzas and €15-20 meals (long hours daily, cash only, immediately across from Savignyplatz S-Bahn entrance, Bleibtreustrasse 49, tel. 030/312-1433).

Zillemarkt Restaurant, which feels like an old-time Berlin *Biergarten,* serves traditional Berlin specialties in the garden or in the rustic candlelit interior. Their *Berliner Allerlei* is a fun way to sample a bit of nearly everything (cabbage, pork, sausage, potatoes, and more for a minimum of two people...but it can feed up to five). They have their own microbrew (€10 meals, daily 10:00-24:00, near the S-Bahn tracks at Bleibtreustrasse 48A, tel. 030/881-7040).

Technische Universität Mensa puts you in a thriving, modern student scene. It feels like a student union building (because it is), with shops, a travel agency, a lounge, kids making out, and lots of international students to chat with. The main cafeteria *(Mensa)* is upstairs—bustling with students and lots of eating options. Streetside is a cafeteria with a more limited selection. Even with the non-student surcharge, eating here is very cheap (€3-6 meals, Mon-Fri 11:00-14:30, closed Sat-Sun, general public entirely welcome but pays the highest of the three prices, coffee bar downstairs with Wi-Fi, just north of Uhlandstrasse at Hardenbergstrasse 34).

Supermarket: The neighborhood grocery store is **Ullrich** (Mon-Sat 9:00-22:00, Sun 11:00-22:00, Kantstrasse 7, under the tracks near Bahnhof Zoo). There's plenty of fast food near Bahnhof Zoo and on Ku'damm.

Near Bahnhof Zoo

Schleusenkrug beer garden is hidden in the park overlooking a canal between the Bahnhof Zoo and Tiergarten stations. Choose from an ever-changing self-service menu of huge salads, pasta, and some German dishes (€7-12 plates, daily 10:00-24:00, food served until 22:00; from Bahnhof Zoo, it's a 5-minute walk, following the path into the park between the zoo and train tracks; tel. 030/313-9909).

Self-Service Cafeterias: The top floor of the famous department store, **KaDeWe,** holds the Winter Garden Buffet view cafeteria, and its sixth-floor deli/food department is a picnicker's nirvana. Its arterials are clogged with more than 1,000 kinds of sausage and 1,500 types of cheese (Mon-Thu 10:00-20:00, Fri 10:00-21:00, Sat 9:30-20:00, closed Sun, U-Bahn: Wittenbergplatz).

Berlin Connections

By Train

Berlin used to have several major train stations. But now that the Hauptbahnhof has emerged as the single, massive central station, all the others have wilted into glorified subway stations. Virtually all long-distance trains pass through the Hauptbahnhof—but it might be under construction again in 2014, with travelers diverted to the Bahnhof Zoo and Ostbahnhof. Before buying a ticket for any long train ride from Berlin (over 7 hours), consider taking a cheap flight instead (buy it well in advance to get a super fare). Train info: tel. 0180-599-6633, www.bahn.com.

EurAide, an agent of Deutsche Bahn (the German railway), sells reservations for high-speed and overnight trains, with staff that can answer your travel questions in English (located in the Hauptbahnhof).

From Berlin by Train to: Potsdam (2/hour, 30 minutes on RE1 train; or take S-Bahn from other points in Berlin, S-7 direct, S-1 with a change at Wannsee, 6/hour, 30-50 minutes), **Oranienburg** and Sachsenhausen Concentration Camp Memorial (hourly, 20 minutes; or take the S-1 line from Friedrichstrasse or other stops in town, 3/hour, 45-50 minutes), **Warnemünde** cruise-ship port (sporadic but roughly every 2 hours, 3.25 hours, most include a transfer in Rostock), **Wittenberg** (a.k.a. *Lutherstadt Wittenberg,* hourly on ICE, 45 minutes; also every 2 hours on slower regional train, 1.25 hours), **Dresden** (every 2 hours, more with a transfer in Leipzig, 2.25 hours), **Leipzig** (hourly direct, 1.25-1.5 hours), **Erfurt** (hourly, 2.5-3 hours, transfer in Leipzig or Naumburg/Saale), **Eisenach** and Wartburg Castle (hourly, 3-3.5 hours, transfer in Leipzig or Naumburg/Saale), **Hamburg** (1-2/hour direct, 1.75-2 hours), **Frankfurt** (hourly, 4 hours), **Bacharach** (hourly, 6.5-7.5 hours, 1-3 changes), **Würzburg** (hourly, 4 hours, change in Göttingen or Fulda), **Rothenburg** (hourly, 5-6 hours, 3 changes), **Nürnberg** (hourly, 4.5 hours), **Munich** (1-2/hour, 6-6.75 hours, every 2 hours direct, otherwise change in Göttingen), **Köln** (hourly, 4.25 hours), **Amsterdam** (roughly hourly to Amsterdam Zuid, 6.5 hours; plus 1 night train/day to Amsterdam Centraal, 9.5 hours), **Budapest** (3/day including one overnight, 11.75-14.25 hours, these go via Czech Republic and Slovakia; if your railpass doesn't cover these countries, save money by going via Vienna—but this route takes longer), **Copenhagen** (8/day, 6.75-8 hours, reservation required, change in Hamburg, 1/day direct departs at 11:25; also consider the direct overnight train-plus-ferry route to Malmö Central Station, Sweden, which is just 20 minutes from Copenhagen— covered by a railpass that includes Germany or Sweden), **London** (8/day, 11-12.75 hours, 2-3 changes—you're better off flying cheap on easyJet or Air Berlin, even if you have a railpass), **Paris** (11/day, 8.75-10 hours, change in Köln—via Belgium—or in Mannheim, 1 direct 13.25-hour night train), **Zürich** (1-2 hour, 8.5-9 hours, transfer in Basel; 1 direct 11-hour night train), **Prague** (6/day direct, 4.75-5.25 hours, 3 overnight trains, 11-13 hours), **Warsaw** (6/day, 5.5-6.5 hours, reservations required on all Warsaw-bound trains), **Kraków** (1/day direct, 10 hours; 2 more with transfer in Warsaw, 8.5 hours), **Vienna** (9/day, most with 1-2 changes, 1/day plus 1/night are direct, 9.75-12 hours; some via Czech Republic, but trains with a change in Nürnberg, Munich, or Würzburg avoid that country—useful if it's not covered by your railpass). It's wise but not required to reserve in advance for trains to or from Amsterdam or Prague.

Night trains run from Berlin to these cities: Munich, Paris, Amsterdam, Vienna, Budapest, Malmö (Sweden, near Copenhagen), Basel, and Zürich. There are no night trains from Berlin to anywhere in Italy or Spain. A *Liegeplatz*, a.k.a. *couchette* berth (€13-36), is a great deal; inquire at EurAide at the Hauptbahnhof for details. Beds generally cost the same whether you have a first- or second-class ticket or railpass. Trains are often full, so reserve your *couchette* a few days in advance from any travel agency or major train station in Europe.

Bus Alternative: Lately, bus travel has become far less expensive than train travel within Germany. If you buy a few days in advance and don't mind a little longer time en route, you can save well over half compared to rail fares. The city's bus station, **ZOB** (Zentraler Omnibusbahnhof), is west of Bahnhof Zoo, in Charlottenburg (Masurenallee 4-6, U2: Kaiserdamm). **Berlin Linien** (www.berlinlinienbus.de) and **Eurolines** (www.eurolines.de) both operate from here to locations around Germany and Europe.

By Plane

Berlin is the continental European hub for budget airlines such as easyJet (lots of flights to Spain, Italy, Eastern Europe, the Baltics, and more—book long in advance to get best fares, www.easyjet.com). Ryanair (www.ryanair.com), Air Berlin (www.airberlin.com), and German Wings (www.germanwings.com) make the London-Berlin trip (and other routes) dirt-cheap, so consider this option before booking an overnight train. Consequently, British visitors to the city are now outnumbered only by Americans.

You'll most likely use **Tegel Airport,** which is four miles from the center (airport code: TXL). Bus #TXL goes between the airport, the Hauptbahnhof (stops by Washingtonplatz entrance), and Alexanderplatz in eastern Berlin. For western Berlin, take bus #X9 to Bahnhof Zoo, or slower bus #109 to Ku'damm and Bahnhof Zoo (€2.40). Bus #128 goes to northern Berlin. A taxi from Tegel Airport costs about €15 to Bahnhof Zoo, or €25 to Alexanderplatz (taxis from Tegel levy a €0.50 surcharge).

Berlin is trying to finish construction of its new airport, **Willy Brandt Berlin-Brandenburg International,** located about 13 miles from central Berlin (airport code: BER; next to the formerly busy Schönefeld Airport). But the project has been perennially delayed; as of this writing, a partial opening in 2014 seems possible but not likely. In case it's open for your visit, here's the scoop: The airport is connected to the city center by fast and frequent Airport Express regional trains (ignore the S-Bahn, as there are no direct S-Bahn trains to the city center; likewise, buses to the U-Bahn lines make little sense for anyone heading straight into central Berlin). The airport station (Flughafen Berlin Brandenburg Bahnhof) sits directly under the terminal, a five-minute walk from the airline check-in desks. To reach my recommended hotels in eastern Berlin, take the RE7 or RB14 to Alexanderplatz (2/hour, 25 minutes, direction: Dessau or Nauen); for my hotels in western Berlin, take either of those trains to Zoologischer Garten (40 minutes). Two additional trains per hour connect the airport to the main train station, via Potsdamer Platz (RE9, 30 minutes). Any train into the city center costs €3 (railpasses valid—but don't activate a flexi-day just for this cheap trip). Buy your ticket at a machine and validate it before boarding by stamping it in one of the nearby boxes. A taxi to the city center costs about €35 (same rates 24/7).

By Cruise Ship (Port of Warnemünde)

Many cruise lines advertise a stop in "Berlin," but the ships actually put in at the Baltic seaside town of Warnemünde—a whopping 150 miles north of downtown Berlin. By train, by tour bus, or by Porsche on the Autobahn, plan on at least three hours of travel time each way between Warnemünde and Berlin. Even if you have a generous 12 to 14 hours in port (as many cruises do here), side-tripping to Berlin means you'll spend about as much time in transit as you will in Berlin itself.

This leads Warnemünde-bound cruisers to the unavoidable question: To Berlin or not to Berlin? If this is your one and only chance to see the German capital, it may well be worth the hassle. With even just five or six hours in Berlin, you can get a good feel for the city. First, follow my self-guided walk from the Reichstag through the Brandenburg Gate and up Unter den Linden. This provides a helpful orientation, and leaves you a couple of hours to grab a quick lunch and visit a museum before heading back to your ship.

Getting to Berlin: You have two good options for making the trip to the city: by train, or on a package tour (one offered by your cruise line or through a third party).

Several **train** connections run each day from Warnemünde to Berlin (typically with a transfer in Rostock). While the schedule can change, in 2013 trains departed Warnemünde at 8:02, 10:02, and 12:02 (all change in Rostock, 3.25 hours total to Berlin); return trains departed Berlin's Hauptbahnhof at 16:43 (change in Rostock, arriving Warnemünde 19:51), 17:26 (direct, arriving Warnemünde 20:10), and 18:44 (change in Rostock, arriving Warnemünde 21:51). Go online to www.bahn.com and check the times for trains between "Warnemuende" and "Berlin Hbf" on the date you'll arrive. Figure €90-106 round-trip for the train.

Warnemünde's train station is a simple 5- to 10-minute walk from the cruise docks: Exit your ship to the right and walk along the water, keeping an eye out for bull's-eye and *City* signs; about 50 yards beyond the car-ferry dock, look for *Tourist Information/Historischer Ortkern* signs on the left. Follow these through the trees and into an underpass that leads to the train station.

An easier but less flexible choice is to pay for a **package excursion.** Cruise lines run trips from Warnemünde into Berlin (typically by bus, though some charter a train). For maximum freedom, opt for a "Berlin On Your Own" excursion—a bus transfer to downtown Berlin with a few unguided hours to explore on your own (generally $150-175). All-day, fully guided bus tours typically cost double ($300-350), but may commit too much time to sights you're not interested in—before you book, carefully read the itinerary specifics. You can also book a tour directly with a local Berlin-based operator; it's worth teaming up with others on your cruise to reduce the per-person cost. For example, **Ship2shore** offers Berlin day trips tailored to your interests starting at €99 per person (based on a minimum of 12 people; smaller groups also possible: €799/2 people, €880/3-4 people, €975/5-6 people, €1,099/6-11 people; tel. 030/243-58058, www.ship2shore.de, info@ship2shore.de). The **Original Berlin Walks** walking-tour company also runs excursions from Warnemünde into Berlin (€760 for up to 3 people in a minibus, €60/additional person up to a maximum of 7).

Staying near Warnemünde: If you'd rather not make the trip to Berlin, you can stick around the port to explore the beach town of Warnemünde and the larger, adjacent city of Rostock. Both towns were part of communist East Germany (DDR), which has left them with some less-than-charming architecture. But today **Warnemünde** is a fun, borderline-tacky seafront resort, with a vast sandy beach and a pretty harbor lined with low-impact diversions. And parts of **Rostock** (a 22-minute train ride away) verge on quaint—it has a fine old church, some museums, and a pedestrian core lined with shops and eateries that cater more to locals than tourists.

For details on both towns—as well as much more detail on how to get into Berlin and spend your time once there—pick up *Rick Steves' Northern European Cruise Ports* guidebook.

NEAR BERLIN

Potsdam • Sachsenhausen Concentration Camp Memorial

While you could spend days in Berlin and not run out of things to do, a few worthwhile side-trips are just outside the city center (within an hour of downtown Berlin). Frederick the Great's opulent palace playground at Potsdam is a hit with those who enjoy ornate interiors and pretty parks. At the opposite end of the city—and the sightseeing spectrum—Sachsenhausen Concentration Camp Memorial provides a somber look at the Nazis' mass production of death during the Holocaust. (A third side-trip possibility—the small town of Wittenberg, with excellent Martin Luther-related sights—is within a 45-minute train ride of Berlin.)

Planning Your Time

Potsdam or Sachsenhausen can take anywhere from a half-day to a full day of your time, depending on your interests. Think twice before visiting Potsdam on a Monday (when Sanssouci Palace is closed) or a Tuesday (when the New Palace is closed); make your pilgrimage to Sachsenhausen any day but Monday (when the grounds are open but interior exhibits are closed).

Potsdam: It takes about an hour one-way from downtown Berlin to reach the palaces at Potsdam (including the train to Potsdam, then a bus to the palaces). The two main palaces—Sanssouci and the New Palace—are quite different but complementary, and connected by a long (30-minute) but pleasant stroll through a park. Visiting either takes about an hour to an hour and a half, plus a potential wait for your Sanssouci entry time (arrive at Sanssouci by 10:00 to avoid waiting in the ticket line). Give yourself five hours round-trip to do the whole shebang. On a quicker visit, you

NEAR BERLIN

can make a beeline from the train station to your choice of palaces (Sanssouci is closer and more intimate, but may require a wait; New Palace is grander but at the far end of the park). It's tempting to stretch your Potsdam visit into a full day so you can linger in the park and tour other royal buildings, poke around the inviting town center of Potsdam, or visit nearby attractions (such as Cecilienhof, the site of the post-WWII Potsdam Conference attended by Churchill, Stalin, and Truman).

If you're an avid cyclist, it's particularly enjoyable to combine a visit to Potsdam with a bike ride along skinny lakes and through green parklands back into the city (rent a bike in Berlin and bring it on the train).

Sachsenhausen: Two hours at the camp is just enough for a quick walk through the grounds; three hours is a minimum if you want to read the many worthwhile exhibits. Factoring in transit time, leave yourself at least six hours round-trip from central Berlin.

Both: For an exhausting day of contrasts, you could get an early start to visit Sachsenhausen (opens at 8:30), munch a picnic lunch on the train down to Potsdam (connected by the S-1 line in about 1.5 hours, with a change at Wannsee; several basic lunch options in Potsdam train station), and tour Frederick the Great's palaces before collapsing on an evening train back to Berlin.

Potsdam

Featuring a lush park strewn with the escapist whimsies of Frederick the Great, the sleepy town of Potsdam has long been Ber-

lin's holiday retreat. It's your best opportunity to get a taste of Prussia's Hohenzollern royalty. While Potsdam's palaces are impressive, they don't quite crack Europe's top 10—perhaps because the audioguides don't inject the Hohenzollerns' personalities into the place (or maybe the Hohenzollerns really were that boring). But Potsdam is convenient to reach from downtown Berlin, and it makes for a great break from the city's heavy history. It's also ideal on a sunny day, thanks to its strolling- and picnic-friendly park.

Getting to Potsdam

Potsdam is about 15 miles southwest of Berlin. You have two easy train options for zipping from the city to Potsdam's Hauptbahnhof (main train station; round-trip covered by €7 Berlin transit day pass with zones ABC). Direct **Regional Express/RE1 trains** depart twice hourly from Berlin's Bahnhof Zoo (20 minutes to Potsdam), Hauptbahnhof (30 minutes), and Friedrichstrasse (35 minutes; any train to Brandenburg or Magdeburg stops in Potsdam). Note: Some RE1 trains continue past the Potsdam Hauptbahnhof to a stop called Park Sanssouci, which is even closer to the palaces (check the schedule).

The **S-Bahn** is slightly slower, but more frequent and handier from some areas of Berlin. The S-7 line goes directly to Potsdam from Alexanderplatz, Hackescher Markt, Friedrichstrasse, Hauptbahnhof, Bahnhof Zoo, and Savignyplatz (6/hour, 30-45 minutes depending on starting point). The S-1 line, which requires a transfer at Wannsee, leaves from Potsdamer Platz, Brandenburger Tor, Friedrichstrasse, Oranienburger Strasse, and other city-center stations; after the line ends at Wannsee, cross the platform to an S-7 train, and ride it three more stops to Potsdam (6/hour, about 45-50 minutes total from downtown Berlin).

Orientation to Potsdam

The city center is enjoyable to explore, but most visitors head right to Frederick the Great's palaces, which surround the gigantic, sprawling Sanssouci Park at the northwest edge of town.

Tourist Information

A handy TI is inside Potsdam's train station (April-Oct Mon-Sat 9:30-20:00, Sun 10:00-16:00; Nov-March Mon-Sat 9:30-18:00, Sun 10:00-16:00; tel. 0331/2755-8830, www.potsdamtourismus. de). Another TI branch, closer to the town center at Luisenplatz, is less convenient for most visitors (April-Oct Mon-Fri 9:30-18:00, Sat-Sun 9:30-16:00; Nov-March Mon-Fri 10:00-18:00, Sat-Sun 9:30-14:00; Brandenburger Strasse 3, tel. 0331/505-8838). Get a map and ask about bus tours if you're interested (see "Tours in Potsdam," later).

The **palace information office** is very helpful, with friendly English-speaking staff. It's across the street from the windmill near the Sanssouci entrance (daily April-Oct 8:30-18:00, Nov-March 8:30-17:00, tel. 0331/969-4200—then press 1, www.spsg. de; clean WC in same building, €0.50).

To supplement the English tour handouts and audioguides at the palaces, consider picking up the blue "official guide" booklets (available individually for each of the sights, €4 apiece at palace information office and gift shops).

Arrival in Potsdam

From Potsdam's **Hauptbahnhof** (main train station), you have several options for reaching the palaces. It's a long (but scenic) 45-minute **walk** (get directions and pick up a map at the TI), or—easier—you can take a bus or tram. To find the bus/tram stops, exit the station toward *Landtag/Friedrich-Engels-Strasse*; this takes you out the main door, where you'll find a row of stops. Various **buses** leave the station about every 10 minutes and connect to either palace (single ride-€1.90, all-day pass-€4, buy tickets at machine on board the bus, also covered by any Berlin pass with zones ABC). The convenient but packed bus #695 cruises through the appealing town center of Potsdam, stopping first at Sanssouci, then at the New Palace (3/hour, 15-20 minutes, leaves from lane 4). Bus #606 only goes to Sanssouci, and bus #605 stops only at the New Palace (3/hour apiece, 10-15 minutes, both leave from lane 5). If you're up for a hike, another option is to take **tram** #91 to Luisenplatz (3/hour, 11 minutes, leaves from lane 1), then walk 20 minutes uphill through the park, which lets you enjoy a classic view of Sanssouci Palace.

If you arrive at Potsdam's **Park Sanssouci Station,** just walk straight out and head up the boulevard called Am Neuen Palais, with the big park on your right-hand side. In about 10 minutes, you'll reach the New Palace.

Tours in Potsdam

Local Tours
The Potsdam TI offers a bus tour of Potsdam sights, plus the interior of Sanssouci Palace. This normally wouldn't be worth considering...except that it's the only way to get into Sanssouci with a live, English-speaking guide (often with some German, too; €28 covers tour, palace, and park in 3.5 hours; April-Oct Tue-Sun at 11:00, no tours Mon or Nov-March; departs from Luisenplatz TI at 11:00 or from train station TI at 11:10; reserve by phone, in summer reserve at least 2 days in advance, tel. 0332/082-1656).

Various bus tours (including hop-on, hop-off options) conveniently connect this town's spread-out sights. Pick up brochures at the TI or check their website (www.potsdamtourismus.de).

Tours from Berlin
Original Berlin Walks, Brewer's Berlin Tours, and other companies offer inexpensive all-day tours from Berlin to Potsdam (1-3/weekly, small groups, English-language only, admissions and public transportation not included, doesn't actually go into Sanssouci Palace). **Original Berlin Walks'** tour leaves Berlin at 9:50 every Sunday from April through October (also on Thu June-Sept; €15, no reservations necessary, meet at taxi stand at Bahnhof Zoo, tel. 030/301-9194, www.berlinwalks.de). The guide takes you to Cecilienhof Palace, through pleasant green landscapes to the historic heart of Potsdam for lunch, and finishes outside Sanssouci Palace. **Brewer's Berlin Tours** depart Berlin at 10:10 on Wednesdays and Saturdays from May through October (€15, no reservations required—just meet at the Bandy Brooks ice cream store at the Friedrichstrasse S-Bahn station, tel. 030/2248-7435, mobile 0177-388-1537, www.brewersberlintours.com).

Sights in Potsdam

Frederick the Great's Palaces
Frederick the Great was a dynamic 18th-century ruler who put Prussia on the map with his merciless military prowess. Yet he also had tender affection for the finer things in life: art, architecture, gardens, literature, and other distin-

guished pursuits. During his reign, Frederick built an impressive ensemble of palaces and other grand buildings around Sanssouci Park, with the two top palaces located at either end. Frederick's super-Rococo Sanssouci Palace is dazzling, while his equally extravagant New Palace was built to wow guests and disprove rumors that Prussia was running out of money after the costly Seven Years' War.

Getting Between the Palaces: It's about a 30-minute walk between Sanssouci and the New Palace. To save time, you can hop on bus #695, which takes you between the palaces in either direction (covered by a cheap €1.30 *Kurzstrecke* ticket, as well as by a Berlin transit pass with zones ABC). If you do walk, you'll find the park wilder, more forested, and less carefully manicured than other big-league European palace complexes (such as Versailles or Vienna's Schönbrunn).

Combo-Ticket: The €19 combo-ticket, covering nearly all the royal buildings in the park, is only worthwhile if you're visiting Sanssouci, New Palace, and at least one other sight (though for most visitors, those two are enough). It's sold only at the Sanssouci Palace ticket office and the New Palace visitors center.

▲▲Sanssouci Palace

Sans souci means "without a care," and this was the carefree summer home of Frederick the Great (built 1745-1747). Of all the palatial

buildings scattered around Potsdam, this was his actual residence. While the palace is small and the audioguide does little to capture the personality of its former resident, it's worth seeing for its opulence.

Cost and Hours: €12, €8 Nov-March, includes audioguide, April-Oct Tue-Sun 10:00-18:00, Nov-March Tue-Sun 10:00-17:00, closed Mon year-round, last entry 30 minutes before closing; in winter (Nov-March), entrance is with a live guided German tour only (departs about every 20 minutes)—about once an hour, they let English speakers with audioguides tag along; tel. 0331/969-4200, www.spsg.de.

Crowd-Beating Tips: At this popular sight, your ticket comes with an appointed entry time. (Tickets are sold for the same day only.) For the most stress-free visit, come early: In the summer, if you arrive by 10:00 (when the ticket office opens), you'll get right in. If you arrive after 11:00, plan to stand in line to buy your ticket. You'll probably have to wait for your entry time, too—usually an hour or two later (pass this time visiting the Ladies' Wing and

Palace Kitchen or exploring the sprawling gardens; if you have a very long wait, zip over to visit the New Palace, then circle back to Sanssouci).

Visiting the Palace: Your ticket covers three parts—The Ladies' Wing (to the left as you face the palace from the front/garden side); the Palace Kitchen (to the right); and the living quarters and festival halls (the main, central part). You can visit the first two sights anytime, but you must report to the main part of the palace at the time noted on your ticket (you'll receive your audioguide there).

The **Ladies' Wing (Damenflügel),** worth a visit only if you have time to kill (and maybe not even then), contains apartments for ladies-in-waiting and servants. Borrow the dull English descriptions and walk past rooms cluttered with cutesy decor. The servants' quarters upstairs have been turned into a painting gallery.

At the **Palace Kitchen (Schlossküche),** see well-preserved mid-19th-century cooking equipment (with posted English information). Hike down the tight spiral staircase to the wine cellar, which features an exhibit about the grapes that were grown on the terraced vineyards out front.

The **Main Palace** was where Frederick the Great spent his summers. The dry audioguide narrates your stroll through the classic Rococo interior, where golden grapevines climb the walls and frame the windows. First explore the Royal Apartments, containing one of Frederick's three libraries (he found it easier to buy extra copies of books rather than move them around), the "study bedroom" where he lived and worked, and the chair where he died. The domed, central Marble Hall resembles the Pantheon in Rome (on a smaller scale), with an oblong oculus, inlaid marble floors, and Corinthian columns made of Carrara marble.

Finally you'll visit the guest rooms, most of which exit straight out onto the delightful terrace. Each room is decorated differently: Chinese, Italian, all yellow, and so on; the niche at the back was for a bed. As you exit (through the servants' quarters), keep an eye out for the giant portrait of Frederick by Andy Warhol.

▲▲New Palace (Neues Palais)

This gigantic showpiece palace (with more than 200 rooms) is, in

some ways, more impressive than the intimate Sanssouci. While Frederick the Great lived primarily at Sanssouci, he built the New Palace later (1763-1769) to host guests and dazzle visiting dignitaries. And unlike at Sanssouci, there's rarely a long wait to buy tickets or enter the palace.

Cost and Hours: €6, includes audioguide, April-Oct Wed-Mon 10:00-18:00, Nov-March Wed-Mon 10:00-17:00, closed Tue year-round, last entry 30 minutes before closing. To see the king's ho-hum apartments—eight small rooms that are a watered-down version of what you'll see at Sanssouci—you must take a required 45-minute tour in German (€5, offered May-Oct daily at 10:00, 11:00, 14:00, and 16:00). During the off-season (Nov-March), the king's apartments are closed, and you can visit the rest of the New Palace by tagging along with a German tour (with an English audioguide; may have to wait up to 30 minutes for next tour). Tel. 0331/969-4200, www.spsg.de.

Visiting the Palace: The tour includes a pair of loaner slippers (to protect the floors) and a one-hour English audioguide that takes you through the ornate halls. From the Grotto Hall, decorated with seashells, you can peer into the lavish Marble Hall, used for fancy gatherings. Continue on through the eight suites of the Lower Princes' Apartments, which accommodated guests and royal family members. In the 19th and early 20th century, German emperors Frederick III (different from the earlier Frederick who built the place) and Wilhelm II (the last Kaiser) resided here. The Gentlemen's Bedchamber holds the red-canopy bed where Kaiser Frederick III died in 1888. The Ladies' Bedchamber is a reminder that noblemen and their wives slept separately.

Upstairs, the Upper Princes' Quarters include a small blue-tiled bathroom that was later installed for Kaiser Wilhelm II. You'll also find Wilhelm's bedroom, as well as a small painting gallery with portraits of Frederick the Great and Russia's Catherine the Great (who was actually a German princess). From up here, you also get a look into the sumptuous, 52-foot-high Marble Hall, with its ceiling painting of the Greek myth of Ganymede and the floors inlaid with Silesian marble. Through the windows, enjoy the views out into the gardens, which recede into the horizon.

Other Palaces

The two main palaces (Sanssouci and the New Palace) are just the beginning. The sprawling Sanssouci Park contains a variety of other

palaces and royal buildings, many of which you can enter. Popular options include the Italian-style **Orangerie** (the last and largest palace in the park, with five royal rooms that must be toured with a German guide, plus a view tower); the **New Chambers** (a royal guest house); the

Chinese House; and other viewpoints, including the **Klausberg Belvedere** and the **Norman Tower.**

Cost and Hours: Each has its own entry fee (€3.50-6; all but Belvedere covered by €19 combo-ticket—see earlier) and hours, some are open weekends only (get a complete list from the Potsdam TI or the palace information office).

Bornstedt Royal Estate (Krongut Bornstedt)

Designed to look like an Italian village, this warehouse-like complex once provided the royal palaces with food and other supplies.

Today the estate houses the Bornstedt Buffalo brewery and distillery, which delivers fine brews and (sometimes) schnapps, as it has since 1689. The brewpub's restaurant is a good place for lunch, serving local specialties (€10-16 plates). The kid-friendly grounds also house a wood-fired bakery with fresh bread and pastries. You can watch hatmakers, candlemakers, coopers, potters, and glassmakers produce (and sell) their wares using traditional techniques.

Cost and Hours: Free except during special events, daily 11:00-19:00, restaurant serves food until 22:00, Ribbeckstrasse 6, tel. 0331/550-650, www.krongut-bornstedt.de.

Getting There: From Sanssouci, walk toward the windmill and follow the street An der Orangerie about 500 yards.

More Sights in Potsdam

Potsdam Town

The easy-to-stroll town center has pedestrianized shopping streets lined with boutiques and eateries. For a small town, this was a cosmopolitan place: Frederick the Great imported some very talented people. For example, Dutch merchants and architects built the Dutch Quarter (Holländisches Viertel, at the intersection of Leiblstrasse and Benkertstrasse) with gabled red-brick buildings that feel like a little corner of Amsterdam. The city also has a good film museum and a museum of Prussian history (both near Breite Strasse). Even if you're just racing through Potsdam on your way to the palaces, you can still catch a glimpse of the town center by riding bus #695 (described earlier, under "Arrival in Potsdam"). Skip Potsdam's much-promoted Wannsee boat rides, which are exceedingly dull.

Cecilienhof

This former residence of Crown Prince William was the site of the historic Potsdam Conference in the summer of 1945. During these meetings, Harry Truman, Winston Churchill, and Joseph Stalin negotiated how best to punish Germany for dragging

Europe through another devastating war. It was here that the postwar map of Europe was officially drawn, setting the stage for a protracted Cold War that would drag on for four and half decades. Designed to appear smaller and more modest than it actually is, Cecilienhof pales in comparison to the grand palaces concentrated around Sanssouci Park; it's only worth visiting if you're a WWII or Cold War history buff (or would like to visit the nearby Meierei brewpub).

Cost and Hours: €6, April-Oct Tue-Sun 10:00-18:00, Nov-March Tue-Sun 10:00-17:00, closed Mon year-round, last entry 30 minutes before closing, tel. 0331/969-4224, www.spsg.de.

Eating: Try the brewery called **Meierei** ("Creamery") at Cecilienhof. Its nice beer garden offers spectacular views of the lake, solid German food, and great homemade beer. When you walk down the hill into the restaurant, note the big open field to the right—it used to be part of the Berlin Wall (€6-15 meals, daily 11:00-22:00, follow *Meierei* signs to Im Neuen Garten 10, tel. 0331/704-3211).

Getting There: Ride the bus to the Reiterweg stop, at the northern end of Potsdam (from Sanssouci Palace, take bus #695; from the train station, ride tram #92 or #96). At Reiterweg, transfer to bus #603 (toward Höhenstrasse), and get off at the Schloss Cecilienhof stop.

Babelsberg

Movie buffs might already know that the nearby suburb of Babelsberg (just east of Potsdam) hosts the biggest film studio in Germany, where classics such as *The Blue Angel* and *Metropolis,* as well as recent hits *The Reader* and *Inglourious Basterds,* were filmed (for information about visiting, see www.filmpark-babelsberg.de).

Sachsenhausen Concentration Camp Memorial

About 20 miles north of downtown Berlin, the small town of Oranienburg was the site of one of the most notorious Nazi concentration camps (which collectively claimed the lives of millions of innocent people). Sachsenhausen's proximity to the capital gave it special status as the place to train camp guards and test new procedures. It was also the site of the Third Reich's massive counterfeiting operation, depicted in the Oscar-winning 2007 movie *The Counterfeiters*. Today Sachsenhausen, worth ▲▲, is open to visitors as a memorial and a museum (Gedenkstätte und Museum Sachsenhausen), honoring the victims and survivors, and teaching visitors about the atrocities that took place here.

Getting There

Take a train to the town of Oranienburg (20-50 minutes); from there, it's a 20-minute walk or a quick trip by bus or taxi to the camp. The whole journey takes just over an hour each way.

From downtown Berlin, a regional train speeds from Hauptbahnhof to Oranienburg (hourly, 20 minutes). Or you can take the S-Bahn (S-1) line from various stops downtown, including Potsdamer Platz, Brandenburger Tor, Friedrichstrasse, and Oranienburger Strasse (3/hour, 45-50 minutes depending on starting point). Note that the slower S-Bahn may not necessarily take longer if you factor in the time it takes to get to the Hauptbahnhof, find the correct platform, and wait for your connecting train. The S-1 line also connects southward to Potsdam (with a change in Wannsee)—making it possible to connect Sachsenhausen and Potsdam's palaces in one extremely busy day.

Once at the Oranienburg train station, it's usually best to **walk** to the memorial (since the bus runs infrequently). It takes about 20 minutes: Turn right out of the train station and head up Stralsunder Strasse for about two blocks. Turn right under the railroad trestle onto Bernauer Strasse, following signs for *Gedenkstätte Sachsenhausen*. At the traffic light, turn left onto André-Pican-Strasse, which becomes Strasse der Einheit. After two blocks, turn right on Strasse der Nationen, where you'll pass a memorial stone commemorating the death march. This leads right to the camp, where you can enter the grounds through the gaps in the wall.

To avoid the walk, take a taxi or catch **bus #804** from in front of the Oranienburg station (hourly, every 2 hours on weekends, lane 4; bus #821 also possible but only 4/day; both covered by Berlin transit pass with zones ABC).

Orientation to Sachsenhausen

Cost and Hours: Free, mid-March-mid-Oct Tue-Sun 8:30-18:00, mid-Oct-mid-March Tue-Sun 8:30-16:30; avoid visiting on Mon, when the grounds and visitors center are open but the exhibits inside the buildings are closed; Strasse der Nationen 22.

Information: The visitors center has WCs, a bookshop, and a helpful information desk. If visiting on your own, pick up the good €0.50 map of the camp. Also consider the €3 audioguide, with up to five hours of commentary (includes map). Tel. 03301/2000, www.gedenkstaette-sachsenhausen.de.

Tours from Berlin: While you can visit Sachsenhausen on your own, a tour helps you understand the camp's complicated and important story. Virtually all walking-tour companies in Berlin offer side-trips to Sachsenhausen. You'll meet in the city, then ride together by train to Oranienburg, and walk to the camp. (Bring along or buy lunch en route, as there's no place to eat at the camp.) The round-trip takes about six hours, much of which is spent in transit—but the time that you spend at the camp is made very meaningful by your guide's commentary.

Check the walking-tour companies' websites, or compare brochures to find an itinerary that fits your schedule. Options include **Original Berlin Walks** (€15, April-Oct Tue-Fri and

Sun at 10:00, runs less frequently off-season) and **Insider Tour** (€15, Tue-Sun at 10:00). Warning: A few unscrupulous tour companies run trips to Sachsenhausen even on Mondays, when the grounds are technically "open," but all of the museum exhibits are closed.

Eating: You can't buy food at the camp. If you need lunch, bring it with you from Berlin, or buy it at the Oranienburg train station.

Background

Completed in July of 1936, Sachsenhausen was the first concentration camp built under SS chief Heinrich Himmler. It was custom-designed in the panopticon ("all-seeing") model popular in British prisons. The grounds were triangular so they could be observed from a single point, the main guard tower. The design was intended to be a model for other camps, but they soon discovered a critical flaw that prevented its widespread adoption: It was very difficult to expand without interfering with sight lines.

Sachsenhausen was not, strictly speaking, a "death camp" for the mass production of murder (like Birkenau); it was a labor camp, intended to wring hard work out of the prisoners. Many toiled in a brickworks, producing materials that were to be used in architect Albert Speer's grandiose plans for erecting new buildings all over Berlin.

Between 1936 and 1945, about 200,000 prisoners did time at Sachsenhausen; about 50,000 died here, while numerous others were transported elsewhere to be killed (in 1942, many of Sachsenhausen's Jews were taken to Auschwitz). Though it was designed to hold 10,000 prisoners, by the end of its functional life the camp had up to 38,000 people. In the spring of 1945, knowing that the Red Army was approaching, guards took 35,000 able-bodied prisoners on a death march, leading them into the forest for seven days and nights with no rations. Rather than "wasting" bullets to kill them, SS troops hoped that the prisoners would ex-

pire from exhaustion. On the eighth day, after 6,000 had already died, the guards abandoned the group in the wilderness, leaving them free. When Soviet troops liberated Sachsenhausen on April 22, 1945, they discovered an additional 3,000 prisoners who had been too weak to walk and were left there to die (all but 300 ended up surviving).

Just three months after the war, Sachsenhausen was converted into a Soviet Special Camp No. 7 for the USSR's own prisoners.

It was a notorious "silent camp," where prisoners would disappear with no information. The prisoners were Nazis as well as anti-Stalin Russians. By the time the camp closed in 1950, 12,000 more prisoners had died here.

In 1961, Sachsenhausen became the first concentration camp turned into a memorial. The East German government did it largely for propaganda purposes: to deflect attention from the controversial construction of the Berlin Wall and to exalt the USSR as the valiant anti-fascist liberators of the camp and all of Germany (rather than to commemorate the victims).

Since the end of communism, the country has redeveloped Sachsenhausen into a true memorial, with updated museum exhibits (scattered throughout the grounds in various buildings) and an emphasis on preservation—documenting and sharing the story of what happened here.

Self-Guided Tour

There's a lot to experience, but this outline covers the basics.

Entrance

First get your bearings in the **visitors center,** where you can peruse the bookshop, buy a map of the grounds, and rent an audioguide.

In the courtyard next to the visitors center, a **model** of the camp illustrates its unique triangular layout, containing the prisoners' barracks. This allowed guards stationed in tower A (at the main gate) to see everything going on inside those three walls. Along the left (east) side of the triangle is the crematorium, called Station Z. (Nazis perversely joked that inmates entered the camp at A and exited at Z.) The smaller buildings outside the main triangle served as workshops, factories, and extra barracks that were added when the camp ran out of room.

Walk up the dusty lane called Camp Street. On the right is the SS officers' R&R building, nicknamed the **"Green Monster,"** where prisoners were forced to dress up and wait on SS officers. Officials mostly chose Jehovah's Witnesses for this duty, because they had a strong pacifist code and could be trusted not to attempt to harm their captors.

Turn left through the fence into the courtyard in front of **guard tower A.** The clock on the tower is frozen at 11:07—the exact time that the Red Army liberated the camp (and a reminder that the Soviets—who were initially responsible for turning the camp into this memorial—were the "good guys"). The building on the right—misnamed the **"New Museum"**—has an interesting DDR-era stained-glass window inside, as well as temporary exhibits and information on Oranienburg Concentration Camp (which in the early 1930s preceded Sachsenhausen as a place for the Nazis to inter political opponents). Nearby is the **SS commandant's house,** which is being turned into a museum about the administration of the camp.

Go through the gate cruelly marked *Arbeit Macht Frei*— "Work will set you free."

Main Grounds

Entering the triangular field, you can see that almost none of the original buildings still stand. Following the war, the Germans

salvaged the barracks here for building materials. Tracing the perimeter, notice the electric fence and barbed wire. A few feet in front of the wall is a gravel track called the **"neutral zone"**—any prisoner setting foot here would be shot. This became a common way for prisoners to attempt suicide. Guards quickly caught on: If they sensed a suicide attempt, they'd shoot to maim instead of kill. It was typical upside-down Nazi logic: Those who wanted to live would die, and those who wanted to die would live.

The daily **roll call** took place in the Appelplatz, the area in front of the guard tower. After a 4:15 wake-up call, prisoners would scramble to eat, bathe, and dress in time for the 5:00 roll call. Dressed in their standard-issue uniforms—thin, striped pajamas and wooden clogs—prisoners would line up while guards, in long coats with angry dogs, barked orders in German and accounted for each person, including those who had died in the barracks overnight. It could take hours, in any weather. One misbehaving prisoner would bring about punishment for all others. One day, after a prisoner escaped, SS officer Rudolf Höss (who later went on to run

Auschwitz-Birkenau) forced the entire population of the camp to stand here for 15 hours in a foot of snow and subzero temperatures. A thousand people died.

To the far right from the entrance, the wooden **barracks** (containing good museum displays and

English descriptions) are reconstructed from original timbers. Barrack 38 focuses on the Jewish experience at Sachsenhausen, as well as the general mistreatment of German Jews under the Nazis (including anti-Semitic propaganda). Barrack 39 explains everyday life, with stories following 20 individual internees. You'll see how prisoners lived: long rows of bunks, benches for taking paltry meals, latrines crammed wall-to-wall with toilets, and communal fountains for washing. Inmates would jockey for access to these facilities. The strongest, meanest, most aggressive prisoners—often here because they had been convicted of a violent crime—would be named *Kapo,* the head of the barrack. This was another example of depraved Nazi logic: The worst prisoners (rather than the best) were "promoted." Like many others, this camp had a prostitution ring—the Nazis brought in female inmates from the women's-only Ravensbrück concentration camp and forced them to "reward good prisoners" at Sachsenhausen.

Next to the barracks is the **camp prison,** where political prisoners or out-of-line inmates were sent. It was run not by the SS, but by the Gestapo (secret police), who would torture captives to extract information. Other prisoners didn't know exactly what went on here, but they could hear howls from inside and knew it was no place they wanted to be. This was also where the Nazis held special hostages, including three Allied airmen who had participated in a bold escape from a Nazi prisoner-of-war camp (the basis for *The Great Escape;* they later managed to escape from Sachsenhausen as well, before being recaptured) and Joseph Stalin's son, Yakov Dzhugashvili, who had been

captured during the fighting at Stalingrad. (The Nazis offered to exchange the young man for five German officers. Stalin refused, and soon after, Yakov died here under mysterious circumstances.) The cells contain exhibits about the prisoners and the methods used by their captors. Outside, you'll find three posts (out of an original 15) with iron pegs near the top. Guards would execute people by tying their hands behind their backs, then hanging them on these pegs by their wrists until they died—a medieval method called *strappado.*

Walk around the semicircle toward the buildings in the middle of the camp. On the gravel **"boot-testing track,"** prisoners were forced to put on boots two sizes too small and walk in a circle all day, supposedly to "test" the shoes for fighting at Stalingrad. The patches of gravel show where each of the barrack buildings once stood. A marker represents the location of the gallows, where prisoners would be publicly executed as a deterrent to others.

Two buildings stand in the middle of the triangle. The one on the left is the **laundry building,** with special exhibits on topics such as Operation Bernhard, Sachsenhausen's counterfeiting ring. Nazi authorities created the world's largest counterfeiting operation by forcing inmates who were skilled forgers to create fake bills that would flood the US and British economies and devalue their currencies. The 2007 movie *The Counterfeiters* depicts the moral dilemma the prisoners faced: Do we create perfect fakes, which will

ultimately work against our own cause? Or do we risk execution by intentionally doing bad work to sabotage the operation?

On the right is the **kitchen building,** with exhibits that trace chronologically the history of the camp. You'll learn how Sachsenhausen was actually built by prisoners, and see original artifacts including the gallows, a bunk from the barracks, uniforms, and so on. There are also photos, quotes, and a 22-minute film. The basement walls feature some bizarre cartoons of vegetables preparing themselves to be eaten (these were drawn later by Soviets).

Memorial and Crematorium

Head back to the far end of the camp, dominated by the towering, 130-foot-tall, 1961 pro-communist DDR **memorial** to the victims of Sachsenhausen. The 18 triangles at the top are red, the color designated for political prisoners (rather than honoring the other Nazi victims who died here). At the base of the monument, two prisoners are being liberated by a noble Soviet soldier. The prisoners are unrealistically robust,

healthy, and optimistic (they will survive and become part of the proud Soviet proletariat!). The **podium** in front was used by the East German army for speeches and rallies—exploiting Sachsenhausen as a backdrop for their propaganda.

Go through the gap in the

fence to find the execution trench, used for mass shootings. Because this system proved too inefficient, the Nazis built Station Z, the **crematorium,** where they could execute and dispose of prisoners more systematically. Prior to the camp's liberation by Soviet troops, Nazi guards destroyed the crematorium to remove evidence of their crimes; the ruins are inside the white building. The ramp took prisoners down into the "infirmary," while the three steps led up to the dressing room. This is where the Nazis tested Zyklon-B (used five times here, this was the chemical responsible for killing hundreds of thousands at Auschwitz). Most of the building's victims died in the room with the double row of bricks (for sound-proofing; the Nazis also blasted classical music to mask noise). Victims would report here for a "dental check," to find out if they had gold or silver teeth that could be taken. They would then stand against the wall to have their height measured—and a guard would shoot them through a small hole in the wall with a single bullet to the back of the skull. (The Nazis found it was easier for guards to

carry out their duties if they didn't have to see their victims face-to-face.)

Bodies were taken to be incinerated in the ovens (which still stand). Notice the statue of the emaciated prisoner—a much more accurate depiction than the one at the DDR monument. Outside, a burial ground is filled with ashes from the crematorium.

The Rest of the Camp

Return to the main part of the camp to visit the remaining sights. You can head left, up to the tip of the triangle (behind the big monument) to find the museum about the postwar era, when Sachsenhausen served as a **Soviet Special Camp**—the often-forgotten second act. Nearby is a burial ground for victims of that camp. At this corner of the triangle, the gate in the fence—called **tower E**—holds a small exhibit about the relationship between the camp and the town of Oranienburg.

Or you can turn right and walk along the wall toward the front corner. The long, green barracks were the **infirmary,** used for medical experiments on inmates (and explained by the exhibits inside). This was also where Soviet soldiers found the 3,000 remaining survivors when they liberated the camp. The small building in back was the morgue—Nazis used the long ramp for wheelbarrows bringing in the day's bodies. Behind that is a field with six stones, each marking 50 bodies for the 300 prisoners who died after the camp was freed.

While all of this is difficult to take in, as with all concentration camp memorials, the intention of Sachsenhausen is to share its story and lessons—and prevent this type of brutality from ever happening again.

PRACTICALITIES

This section covers just the basics on traveling in Germany (for much more information, see *Rick Steves' Germany*). You can find free advice on specific topics at www.ricksteves.com/tips.

Money

Germany uses the euro currency: 1 euro (€) = about $1.30. To convert prices in euros to dollars, add about 30 percent: €20 = about $26, €50 = about $65. (Check www.oanda.com for the latest exchange rates.)

The standard way for travelers to get euros is to withdraw money from ATMs (which locals call a *Geldautomat*) using a debit card, ideally with a Visa or MasterCard logo. Before departing, call your bank or credit-card company: Confirm that your card(s) will work overseas, ask about international transaction fees, and alert them that you'll be making withdrawals in Europe. Also ask for the PIN number for your credit card in case it'll help you use Europe's "chip-and-PIN" payment machines (see below); allow time for your bank to mail your PIN to you. To keep your valuables safe, wear a money belt.

Dealing with "Chip and PIN": Much of Europe—including Germany—is adopting a "chip-and-PIN" system for credit cards, and some merchants rely on it exclusively. European chip-and-PIN cards are embedded with an electronic chip, in addition to the magnetic stripe used on our American-style cards. This means that your credit (and debit) card might not work at payment machines, such as those at train and subway stations, toll roads, parking garages, luggage lockers, and self-serve gas pumps. Memorizing your credit card's PIN lets you use it at some chip-and-PIN machines—just enter your PIN when prompted. If a payment machine won't take your card, look for a machine that takes cash or see if there's a cashier nearby who can process your transaction.

Often the easiest solution is to pay for your purchases with cash you've withdrawn from an ATM using your debit card (Europe's ATMs still accept magnetic-stripe cards).

Phoning

Smart travelers use the telephone to reserve or reconfirm rooms, reserve restaurants, get directions, research transportation connections, confirm tour times, phone home, and lots more.

To call Germany from the US or Canada: Dial 011-49 and then the area code (minus its initial zero) and local number. (The 011 is our international access code, and 49 is Germany's country code.)

To call Germany from a European country: Dial 00-49 followed by the area code (minus its initial zero) and local number. (The 00 is Europe's international access code.)

To call within Germany: If you're dialing within an area code, just dial the local number; but if you're calling outside your area code, you have to dial both the area code (which starts with a 0) and the local number.

To call from Germany to another country: Dial 00 followed by the country code (for example, 1 for the US or Canada), then the area code and number. If you're calling European countries whose phone numbers begin with 0, you'll usually have to omit that 0 when you dial.

Tips on Phoning: Local phone numbers in Germany can have different numbers of digits within the same city or even the same business. Mobile phone numbers start with 015, 016, or 017, and cost much more to call than land lines.

A mobile phone—whether an American one that works in Germany, or a European one you buy upon arrival—is handy, but can be pricey. If traveling with a smartphone, switch off data-roaming until you have free Wi-Fi. With Wi-Fi, you can use your smartphone to make free or inexpensive domestic and international calls by taking advantage of a calling app such as Skype or FaceTime.

To make cheap international calls from any phone (even your hotel-room phone), you can buy an international phone card. These work with a scratch-to-reveal PIN code, allow you to call home to the US for pennies a minute, and also work for domestic calls. Avoid using international phone cards at pay phones. Because the German phone company slaps on hefty surcharges, you'll get far fewer minutes for your money (for example, 10 minutes instead of 100 on a €5 card) than if you call from your hotel room.

Another option is buying an insertable phone card. These are usable only at pay phones, are reasonable for making calls within the country, and work for international calls as well (though not

From: rick@ricksteves.com
Sent: Today
To: info@hotelcentral.com
Subject: Reservation request for 19-22 July

Dear Hotel Central,

I would like to reserve a room for 2 people for 3 nights, arriving 19 July and departing 22 July. If possible, I would like a quiet room with a double bed and a bathroom inside the room.

Please let me know if you have a room available and the price.

Thank you!
Rick Steves

as cheaply as the international phone cards). Note that insertable phone cards—and most international phone cards—work only in the country where you buy them.

Calling from your hotel-room phone is usually expensive, unless you use an international phone card. For much more on phoning, see www.ricksteves.com/phoning.

Making Hotel Reservations

To ensure the best value, I recommend reserving rooms in advance, particularly during peak season. Email the hotelier with the following key pieces of information: number and type of rooms; number of nights; date of arrival; date of departure; and any special requests. (For a sample form, see the sidebar.) Use the European style for writing dates: day/month/year. Hoteliers typically ask for your credit-card number as a deposit.

Given the economic downturn, hoteliers may be willing to make a deal—try emailing several hotels to ask for their best price. In general, hotel prices can soften if you do any of the following: offer to pay cash, stay at least three nights, or travel off-season.

Eating

At mealtime, there are many options beyond restaurants. For hearty, stick-to-the-ribs meals—and plenty of beer—look for a beer hall *(Bräuhaus)* or beer garden *(Biergarten)*. Gasthaus, Gasthof, Gaststätte, and Gaststube all loosely describe an informal, inn-type eatery. A *Kneipe* is a bar, and a *Keller* (or *Ratskeller*) is a restaurant or tavern located in a cellar. A *Schnell Imbiss* is a small fast-food take-away stand. Department-store cafeterias are also common and handy.

The classic German dish is sausage *(Wurst)*. The hundreds of varieties are usually served with mustard *(Senf)*, a roll *(Semmel)* or pretzel *(Breze)*, and sauerkraut. The various types of *Bratwurst* are

PRACTICALITIES

grilled *(gebraten)*. To enjoy a *Weisswurst*—a boiled white Bavarian sausage made of veal—peel off the skin and eat it with sweet mustard. *Currywurst* comes with a delicious curry-infused ketchup. You'll also find schnitzel everywhere (pork is cheaper than veal). Salads are big, leafy, and good. Germans are passionate about choosing organic products—look for *Bio*.

Ethnic eateries—such as Italian, Turkish, Greek, and Asian—are good values. Shops and stands selling Turkish-style *Döner Kebab* (gyro-like, pita-wrapped rotisserie meat) are also common.

In Germany, good service is relaxed (slow to an American). When you want the bill, say, *"Rechnung* (REHKH-noong), *bitte."* To tip for good service, it's customary to round up around 10 percent. Rather than leave coins on the table, do as the locals do: When you pay, tell the waiter how much you want him to keep, including his tip. For example, for a €10 meal, you can hand over a €20 bill and say *"Elf Euro"*—"Eleven euros"—to include a €1 tip and get €9 change.

Germany has both great wine *(Wein)* and beer *(Bier)*. Order wine *süss* (sweet), *halb trocken* (medium), or *trocken* (dry). For beer, *dunkles* is dark, *helles* or *Lager* is light, *Flaschenbier* is bottled, and *vom Fass* is on tap. *Pils* is barley-based, and *Weizen, Hefeweizen,* or *Weissbier* is yeasty and wheat-based. When you order beer, ask for *eine Halbe* for a half-liter (though it's not always available) or *eine Mass* for a whole liter (about a quart).

Transportation

By Train: German trains—speedy, comfortable, non-smoking, and fairly punctual—cover cities and small towns well. Faster trains (such as the high-speed ICE) are more expensive than slower "regional" trains. To see if a railpass could save you money—which is often the case in Germany—check www.ricksteves.com/rail. If buying point-to-point tickets, note that prices can fluctuate (you can usually save money by booking more expensive train journeys online; tickets are sold up to three months in advance). To research train schedules and fares, visit Germany's excellent online timetable, www.bahn.com.

By Car: It's cheaper to arrange most car rentals from the US. For tips on your insurance options, see www.ricksteves.com/cdw, and for route planning, consult www.viamichelin.com. Bring your driver's license. Germany's toll-free autobahn (freeway) system lets you zip around the country in a snap. While there's often no official speed limit, going above the posted recommended speed invalidates your insurance. Many German cities—including Munich, Freiburg, Frankfurt, Köln, Dresden, Leipzig, and Berlin—require drivers to buy a special sticker *(Umweltplakette)* to drive in the city center. These already come standard with most German rental cars; ask when you pick up your car. A car is a worthless headache in cities—park it safely (get tips from your hotel).

Local road etiquette is similar to that in the US. Ask your car-rental company about the rules of the road, or check the US State Department website (www.travel.state.gov, click on "International Travel," then specify your country of choice and click "Traffic Safety and Road Conditions").

Helpful Hints

Emergency Help: To summon the **police** or an **ambulance,** call 112. For passport problems, call the **US Embassy** (in Berlin, tel. 030/83050, consular services tel. 030/8305-1200—Mon–Thu 14:00–16:00 only) or the **Canadian Embassy** (in Berlin, tel. 030/203-120). For other concerns, get advice from your hotel.

Theft or Loss: To replace a passport, you'll need to go in person to an embassy (see above). Cancel and replace your credit and debit cards by calling these 24-hour US numbers collect: Visa—tel. 303/967-1096, MasterCard—tel. 636/722-7111, American Express—tel. 336/393-1111. File a police report either on the spot or within a day or two; you'll need it to submit an insurance claim for lost or stolen railpasses or travel gear, and it can help with replacing your passport or credit and debit cards. Precautionary measures can minimize the effects of loss—back up your digital photos and other files frequently. For more information, see www.ricksteves.com/help.

Time: Germany uses the 24-hour clock. It's the same through 12:00 noon, then keep going: 13:00, 14:00, and so on. Germany, like most of continental Europe, is six/nine hours ahead of the East/West Coasts of the US.

Business Hours: In Germany, most shops are open from about 9:00 until 18:00 or 20:00 on weekdays, but close early on Saturday (generally between 12:00 and 17:00, depending on whether you're in a town or a big city). In small towns, a few shops may take a mid-afternoon break on weekdays (roughly between 12:00 and 14:00 or 15:00). Throughout Germany, most shops close entirely on Sundays.

Holidays and Festivals: Germany celebrates many holidays, which can close sights and attract crowds (book hotel rooms ahead). For more on holidays and festivals, check Germany's website: www.germany.travel. For a simple list showing major—though not all—events, see www.ricksteves.com/festivals.

Numbers and Stumblers: What Americans call the second floor of a building is the first floor in Europe. Europeans write dates as day/month/year. Commas are decimal points and vice versa—a dollar and a half is 1,50, and there are 5.280 feet in a mile.

Germany uses the metric system: A kilogram is 2.2 pounds; a liter is about a quart; and a kilometer is six-tenths of a mile.

Resources from Rick Steves

This Snapshot guide is excerpted from my latest edition of *Rick Steves' Germany*, which is one of more than 30 titles in my series of guidebooks on European travel. I also produce a public television series, *Rick Steves' Europe*, and a public radio show, *Travel with Rick Steves*. My website, www.ricksteves.com, offers free travel information, a forum for travelers' comments, guidebook updates, my travel blog, an online travel store, and information on European railpasses and our tours of Europe. If you're bringing a mobile device on your trip, you can download free information from Rick Steves Audio Europe, featuring podcasts of my radio shows, free audio tours of major sights in Europe, and travel interviews about Germany (via www.ricksteves.com/audioeurope, iTunes, Google Play, or the Rick Steves Audio Europe free smartphone app). You can follow me on Facebook and Twitter.

Additional Resources

Tourist Information: www.germany.travel
Passports and Red Tape: www.travel.state.gov
Packing List: www.ricksteves.com/packlist
Travel Insurance: www.ricksteves.com/insurance
Cheap Flights: www.kayak.com
Airplane Carry-on Restrictions: www.tsa.gov/travelers
Updates for This Book: www.ricksteves.com/update

How Was Your Trip?

If you'd like to share your tips, concerns, and discoveries after using this book, please fill out the survey at www.ricksteves.com/feedback. Thanks in advance—it helps a lot.

German Survival Phrases

In the phonetics, ī sounds like the long i in "light," and bolded syllables are stressed.

English	German	Pronunciation
Good day.	Guten Tag.	**goo**-tehn tahg
Do you speak English?	Sprechen Sie Englisch?	**shprehkh**-ehn zee **ehgn**-lish
Yes. / No.	Ja. / Nein.	yah / nīn
I (don't) understand.	Ich verstehe (nicht).	ikh fehr-**shtay**-heh (nikht)
Please.	Bitte.	**bit**-teh
Thank you.	Danke.	**dahng**-keh
I'm sorry.	Es tut mir leid.	ehs toot meer līt
Excuse me.	Entschuldigung.	ehnt-**shool**-dig-oong
(No) problem.	(Kein) Problem.	(kīn) proh-**blaym**
(Very) good.	(Sehr) gut.	(zehr) goot
Goodbye.	Auf Wiedersehen.	owf **vee**-der-zayn
one / two	eins / zwei	īns / tsvī
three / four	drei / vier	drī / feer
five / six	fünf / sechs	fewnf / zehkhs
seven / eight	sieben / acht	**zee**-behn / ahkht
nine / ten	neun / zehn	noyn / tsayn
How much is it?	Wieviel kostet das?	**vee**-feel **kohs**-teht dahs
Write it?	Schreiben?	**shrī**-behn
Is it free?	Ist es umsonst?	ist ehs oom-**zohnst**
Included?	Inklusive?	in-kloo-**zee**-veh
Where can I buy / find...?	Wo kann ich kaufen / finden...?	voh kahn ikh **kow**-fehn / **fin**-dehn
I'd like / We'd like...	Ich hätte gern / Wir hätten gern...	ikh **heh**-teh gehrn / veer **heh**-tehn gehrn
...a room.	...ein Zimmer.	īn **tsim**-mer
...a ticket to ____.	...eine Fahrkarte nach ____.	ī-neh **far**-kar-teh nahkh
Is it possible?	Ist es möglich?	ist ehs **mur**-glikh
Where is...?	Wo ist...?	voh ist
...the train station	...der Bahnhof	dehr **bahn**-hohf
...the bus station	...der Busbahnhof	dehr **boos**-bahn-hohf
...the tourist information office	...das Touristen- informations- büro	dahs too-**ris**-tehn- in-for-maht-see-**ohns**- bew-roh
...toilet	...die Toilette	dee toh-**leh**-teh
men	Herren	**hehr**-rehn
women	Damen	**dah**-mehn
left / right	links / rechts	links / rehkhts
straight	geradeaus	geh-**rah**-deh-ows
When is this...	Um wieviel Uhr ist hier...	oom **vee**-feel oor ist heer
...open / closed?	...geöffnet / geschlossen?	geh-**urf**-neht / geh-**shloh**-sehn
At what time?	Um wieviel Uhr?	oom **vee**-feel oor
Just a moment.	Moment.	moh-**mehnt**
now / soon / later	jetzt / bald / später	yehtst / bahld / **shpay**-ter
today / tomorrow	heute / morgen	**hoy**-teh / **mor**-gehn

PRACTICALITIES

In the Restaurant

English	German	Pronunciation
I'd like / We'd like...	Ich hätte gern / Wir hätten gern...	ikh **heh**-teh gehrn / veer **heh**-tehn gehrn
...a reservation for...	...eine Reservierung für...	ī-neh reh-zer-**feer**-oong fewr
...a table for one / two.	...einen Tisch für eine Person / zwei Personen.	ī-nehn tish fewr ī-neh pehr-zohn / tsvī pehr-**zoh**-nehn
Non-smoking.	Nichtraucher.	**nikht**-rowkh-er
Is this seat free?	Ist hier frei?	ist heer frī
Menu (in English), please.	Speisekarte (auf Englisch), bitte.	**shpī**-zeh-kar-teh (owf **ehng**-lish) **bit**-teh
service (not) included	Trinkgeld (nicht) inklusive	**trink**-gehlt (nikht) in-kloo-**zee**-veh
cover charge	Eintritt	**īn**-trit
to go	zum Mitnehmen	tsoom **mit**-nay-mehn
with / without	mit / ohne	mit / **oh**-neh
and / or	und / oder	oont / **oh**-der
menu (of the day)	(Tages-) Karte	(**tah**-gehs-) **kar**-teh
set meal for tourists	Touristenmenü	too-**ris**-tehn-meh-**new**
specialty of the house	Spezialität des Hauses	shpayt-see-ah-lee-**tayt** dehs **how**-zehs
appetizers	Vorspeise	**for**-shpī-zeh
bread / cheese	Brot / Käse	broht / **kay**-zeh
sandwich	Sandwich	**zahnd**-vich
soup	Suppe	**zup**-peh
salad	Salat	zah-**laht**
meat	Fleisch	flīsh
poultry	Geflügel	geh-**flew**-gehl
fish	Fisch	fish
seafood	Meeresfrüchte	**meh**-rehs-**frewkh**-teh
fruit	Obst	ohpst
vegetables	Gemüse	geh-**mew**-zeh
dessert	Nachspeise	**nahkh**-shpī-zeh
mineral water	Mineralwasser	min-eh-**rahl**-vah-ser
tap water	Leitungswasser	**lī**-toongs-vah-ser
milk	Milch	milkh
(orange) juice	(Orangen-) Saft	(oh-**rahn**-zhehn-) zahft
coffee / tea	Kaffee / Tee	kah-**fay** / tay
wine	Wein	vīn
red / white	rot / weiß	roht / vīs
glass / bottle	Glas / Flasche	glahs / **flah**-sheh
beer	Bier	beer
Cheers!	Prost!	prohst
More. / Another.	Mehr. / Noch eins.	mehr / nohkh īns
The same.	Das gleiche.	dahs **glīkh**-eh
Bill, please.	Rechnung, bitte.	**rehkh**-noong **bit**-teh
tip	Trinkgeld	**trink**-gehlt
Delicious!	Lecker!	**lehk**-er

For more user-friendly German phrases, check out *Rick Steves' German Phrase Book and Dictionary* or *Rick Steves' French, Italian & German Phrase Book.*

INDEX

INDEX

INDEX

Rick's Free Travel App

Get your FREE **Rick Steves Audio Europe**™ app to enjoy…

- Dozens of self-guided tours of Europe's top museums, sights and historic walks

- Hundreds of tracks filled with cultural insights and sightseeing tips from Rick's radio interviews

- All organized into handy geographic playlists

- For iPhone, iPad, iPod Touch, Android

With Rick whispering in your ear, Europe gets even better.

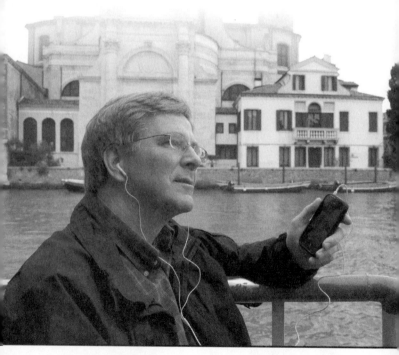

Find out more at ricksteves.com

Free information and great gear to

▸ Explore Europe

Browse thousands of articles, video clips, photos and radio interviews, plus find a wealth of money-saving tips for planning your dream trip. You'll find up-to-date information on Europe's best destinations, packing smart, getting around, finding rooms, staying healthy, avoiding scams and more.

▸ Travel News

Subscribe to our free Travel News e-newsletter, and get monthly updates from Rick on what's happening in Europe!

▸ Travel Forums

Learn, ask, share—our online community of savvy travelers is a great resource for first-time travelers to Europe, as well as seasoned pros.

Rick Steves' Europe Through the Back Door, Inc

turn your travel dreams into affordable reality

▶ Rick's Free Audio Europe™ App

The Rick Steves Audio Europe™ app brings history and art to life. Enjoy Rick's audio tours of Europe's top museums, sights and neighborhood walks—plus hundreds of tracks including travel tips and cultural insights from Rick's radio show—all organized into geographic playlists. Learn more at ricksteves.com.

▶ Great Gear from Rick's Travel Store

Pack light and right—on a budget—with Rick's custom-designed carry-on bags, wheeled bags, day packs, travel accessories, guidebooks, journals, maps and Blu-ray/DVDs of his TV shows.

130 Fourth Avenue North, PO Box 2009 • Edmonds, WA 98020 USA
Phone: (425) 771-8303 • Fax: (425) 771-0833 • ricksteves.com

NOW AVAILABLE:
eBOOKS, DVD & BLU-RAY

TRAVEL CULTURE
Europe 101
European Christmas
Postcards from Europe
Travel as a Political Act

eBOOKS
Nearly all Rick Steves guides are available as eBooks. Check with your favorite bookseller.

RICK STEVES' EUROPE DVDs
11 New Shows 2013–2014
Austria & the Alps
Eastern Europe
England & Wales
European Christmas
European Travel Skills & Specials
France
Germany, BeNeLux & More
Greece, Turkey & Portugal
Iran
Ireland & Scotland
Italy's Cities
Italy's Countryside
Scandinavia
Spain
Travel Extras

BLU-RAY
Celtic Charms
Eastern Europe Favorites
European Christmas
Italy Through the Back Door
Mediterranean Mosaic
Surprising Cities of Europe

PHRASE BOOKS & DICTIONARIES
French
French, Italian & German
German
Italian
Portuguese
Spanish

JOURNALS
Rick Steves' Pocket Travel Journal
Rick Steves' Travel Journal

PLANNING MAPS
Britain, Ireland & London
Europe
France & Paris
Germany, Austria & Switzerland
Ireland
Italy
Spain & Portugal

Rick Steves books and DVDs are available at bookstores and through online booksellers.

Rick Steves®

www.ricksteves.com

EUROPE GUIDES

Best of Europe
Eastern Europe
Europe Through the Back Door
Mediterranean Cruise Ports
Northern European Cruise Ports

COUNTRY GUIDES

Croatia & Slovenia
England
France
Germany
Great Britain
Ireland
Italy
Portugal
Scandinavia
Spain
Switzerland

CITY & REGIONAL GUIDES

Amsterdam, Bruges & Brussels
Barcelona
Budapest
Florence & Tuscany
Greece: Athens & the Peloponnese
Istanbul
London
Paris
Prague & the Czech Republic
Provence & the French Riviera
Rome
Venice
Vienna, Salzburg & Tirol

SNAPSHOT GUIDES

Berlin
Bruges & Brussels
Copenhagen & the Best of
    Denmark
Dublin
Dubrovnik
Hill Towns of Central Italy
Italy's Cinque Terre
Krakow, Warsaw & Gdansk
Lisbon
Madrid & Toledo
Milan & the Italian Lakes District
Munich, Bavaria & Salzburg
Naples & the Amalfi Coast
Northern Ireland
Norway
Scotland
Sevilla, Granada & Southern Spain
Stockholm

POCKET GUIDES

Athens
Barcelona
Florence
London
Paris
Rome
Venice

Rick Steves guidebooks are published by Avalon Travel,
a member of the Perseus Books Group.

Avalon Travel
a member of the Perseus Books Group
1700 Fourth Street
Berkeley, CA 94710

Printed in Canada by Friesens. First printing January 2014.

ISBN 978-1-61238-692-8

For the latest on Rick's lectures, guidebooks, tours, public radio show, and public television series, contact Europe Through the Back Door, Box 2009, Edmonds, WA 98020,
tel. 425/771-8303, fax 425/771-0833, www.ricksteves.com, rick@ricksteves.com.

Europe Through the Back Door
Managing Editor: Risa Laib
Editorial & Production Manager: Jennifer Madison Davis
Editors: Glenn Eriksen, Tom Griffin, Cameron Hewitt, Deb Jensen, Suzanne Kotz,
    Cathy Lu, John Pierce, Carrie Shepard
Editorial Assistant: Jessica Shaw
Editorial Intern: Zosha Millman
Researchers: Glenn Eriksen, Cameron Hewitt, Cary Walker, Ian Watson
Maps & Graphics: David C. Hoerlein, Sandra Hundacker, Lauren Mills, Mary
    Rostad, Laura VanDeventer

Avalon Travel
Senior Editor and Series Manager: Madhu Prasher
Editor: Jamie Andrade
Associate Editor: Annette Kohl
Assistant Editor: Maggie Ryan
Copy Editor: Suzie Nasol
Proofreader: Gayle Hart
Indexer: Stephen Callahan
Production & Typesetting: McGuire Barber Design
Cover Design: Kimberly Glyder Design
Maps & Graphics: Kat Bennett, Mike Morgenfeld

Front Cover Photo: Brandenburg gate at sunset, Berlin © Sborisov | Dreamstime.com
Title Page Photo: view of the French Cathedral and the Konzerthaus at Gendarmenmarkt
    © Heike Jestram/www.123rf.com
Page 1 Photo: Kaiser Wilhelm Memorial Church © www.123rf.com
Additional Photography: Dominic Bonuccelli, Lee Evans, Cameron Hewitt, David C.
    Hoerlein, Robyn Stencil, Rick Steves, Gretchen Strauch, Karoline Vass, Ian Watson

ABOUT THE AUTHOR

RICK STEVES

Since 1973, Rick Steves has spent 100 days every year exploring Europe. Along with writing and researching a bestselling series of guidebooks, Rick produces a public television series *(Rick Steves' Europe)*, a public radio show *(Travel with Rick Steves)*, and an app and podcast *(Rick Steves Audio Europe)*; writes a nationally syndicated newspaper column; organizes guided tours that take over ten thousand travelers to Europe annually; and offers an information-packed website (www.ricksteves.com). With the help of his hardworking staff of 80 at Europe Through the Back Door—in Edmonds, Washington, just north of Seattle—Rick's mission is to make European travel fun, affordable, and culturally enlightening for Americans.

Connect with Rick:

facebook.com/RickSteves twitter: @RickSteves

More for your trip!
Maximize the experience with Rick Steves as your guide

Guidebooks
Switzerland, Vienna and Prague guides make side-trips smooth and affordable

Phrase Books
Rely on Rick's German Phrase Book & Dictionary

Rick's DVDs and Blu-rays
Preview where you're going with 4 shows on Germany

Free! Rick's Audio Europe™ App
Hear free Germany travel tips from Rick's radio shows

Small-Group Tours
Including the Best of Germany, Austria and Switzerland

For all the details, visit ricksteves.com